God

MORE THAN JUST A NAME

God

MORE THAN JUST A NAME

cecil murphey

BROADMAN
&HOLMAN
PUBLISHERS

Nashville, Tennessee

0–8054–2337–0

Published by Broadman & Holman Publishers, Nashville, Tennessee

Dewey Decimal Classification: 231
Subject Heading: CHRISTIAN DOCTRINE

Library of Congress Cataloging-in-Publication Data

Murphey, Cecil B.
    God—more than just a name / Cecil Murphey.
    p.   cm.
    ISBN 0–8054–2337–0 (pbk.)
    God. I. Title.

BT102 .M853 2001
231—dc21

2001035257

1 2 3 4 5 6 7 8 9 10   05 04 03 02 01

Dedication

So many have shaped my understanding of God, but especially I want to thank Joan and Maurice Wheatley.

My deep appreciation to Alan Ross and Phyllis Rice because they know how to sponsor champions.

Many thanks to my agent Deidre Knight, who suggested that I write this book and who constantly encourages me. I add my sincere thanks to my editor Len Goss for his enthusiastic acceptance and skillful editing.

I'm grateful to several people in the writing profession for their kindness to me as they live out the theology they teach: Marlene Bagnull, Mike Brewer, Sandy Brooks, Elaine Colvin, Reg and Eleonore Forder, Mona Hodgson, Wayne Holmes, Lin Johnson, Virelle Kidder, Steve Laube, Yvonne Lehman, Susan Osborn, Michael Smith, Sally Stuart, and Jim Watkins.

My deepest thanks to Shirley—God's special and totally undeserved gift to me.

Contents

∞

Read This First: An Introduction

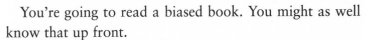

You're going to read a biased book. You might as well know that up front.

The truth is, none of us writes objectively. It becomes most obvious when we read those who, blinded by their prejudices, deny their preferences and insist they look only at the relevant facts. But even that statement is subjective. Whenever we write, talk, investigate, or even think, we ignore or rule out certain things and confine ourselves to a limited number of sources. When we decide what is relevant, that's prejudice at work.

I've decided to tell readers on the first page where I draw the lines. From here on, anything you read will be shaped by my limited understanding of an unlimited topic—God.

I come from a middle-of-the-road, evangelical, Protestant background. I teach an adult Sunday school class. I'm one of those people who goes to church every week and wouldn't consider not going. I often say, "The church can get along without me, but I can't get along without the church."

To say it even clearer: I view the Bible as inspired by God. Like the Reformers of old, the Bible is my guide of "faith and practice."

God: More Than Just a Name begins by limiting the scope of investigation to the Bible—the primary source from which we learn about God. (If you didn't get it before, in that last statement you read my bias.)

As I see it, the God of the Bible isn't the *object* of human search; it's the *subject*. This means that the Bible isn't a book of history, science, or literature. It's a book about the faith of the people of God. Each story, narrative, and command points to the God who is initially unknown and is gradually revealed through active intervention in human lives.

Like the Bible itself, I make no effort to prove God's existence. The holy Book affirms that God is and that God actively works in our world. In fact, the first words of the Bible are "in the beginning, God created the heavens and the earth" (Gen. 1:1). That's precisely where I start.

Not only do I not attempt to argue for divine existence, but I rely on the Bible as the primary source of revelation about God.

The Bible is a book about a God who seeks an intimate relationship with humanity and who starts with one nation—Israel—as the means to that end. For me, as a follower of Jesus Christ, the culmination of God's activities finds fulfillment in the New Testament. The writings of the Old Testament point to Jesus not only as God's human representation on earth, but even more as God's ultimate act of love and grace in reaching out to human pain and isolation.

∞

As a final statement on my bias, I'm one of those adult converts to the faith. Other than an occasional visit in childhood, I didn't go inside a church until I was in my early twenties.

My visit to a house of God was prompted by a personal need. I had ended a sad love affair (I was dumped!) and I was hurting. I remember thinking that there must be more to life than birth, death at the end, and a lot of ups and downs in between. I began to ask what philosophers called the existential question: What does life mean?

In my pain, I turned to God. And I wasn't disappointed.

My intention is simply to tell you about the God of the Bible as objectively as I can with my given prejudices.

CHAPTER I

The Gender of God

———————— ∞ ————————

I get jokes via e-mail regularly. One of them I received was children's questions to God. A girl, age nine, wrote, "I know you're a boy, but can you be fair anyway?"

Cute? Of course. But it's also sad. It said that at nine years of age she had already "learned" that God is male, and therefore, like other males.

I wish I could talk to her. The first thing I would say is this: God is a Spirit. Jesus said it (John 4:24), and so did the prophets. Not many people believe God is some white-haired old man with a white, flowing robe. That is, they say they don't.

OK, so is God male? The Bible never says so.

The problem of God's gender is linguistic. How do we speak of an all-powerful, all-knowing, all-seeing God who is neither male nor female? To think of God in some neuter sense doesn't seem to fit either.

Biblical writers used the masculine pronoun when speaking about God. Males ruled the ancient world—

what we call a patriarchal society. To call God "he" is a sensible way to speak of God. Yet the word for *spirit* is neuter. Traditionally, scholars have had trouble with this. How could Spirit be nongendered if God is male?

Recent translators have struggled to avoid the masculine pronoun without sounding awkward. It's not easy to do! With few exceptions, they have continued to use "he" and "him." The biblical quotations in this book reflect that problem, and God gets the masculine pronoun.

CHAPTER 2

God's Most Important Name

How can we know God? Although many people have posed the question, the answer has always been the same. We know God because of divine self-revelation to the human race. Those self-revelations came to us through the Book of God—the holy Bible. (*Bible* is a transliteration of the Greek word for *books*.) When we look at the holy Book, we find that God was revealed to the human race through a variety of actions. But, perhaps even more, we can learn to understand more about God through the self-disclosed names.

Ancient Jews would never have asked, "Who is God?" and expect a name. Instead, they would have asked, "What does God *do?*" Not only is Hebrew a language built on verbs instead of nouns, but this underscores the Jewish approach to God. They grasped the divine nature by observing and participating in the activities of God. Therefore, they would define the Almighty by speaking of "the Healing One" or "the Providing One."

By contrast, ancient Greeks, with a language built on nouns, seized on the is-ness of God. Their more static definitions would say, "God *is* holy" or "God *is* love." Centuries later, most of those who wrote creeds for the church followed the Greek way of thinking.

The Most Important Name of God

Of all the self-revealing names, one stands out above all the others. It is the name limited and applied only to the chosen people—the Jews. We sometimes call it the personal name of God, and certainly it is the most special of all names.

Unfortunately, no one knows what it is!

It's not quite that bad. We don't know how to spell it and, consequently, we don't know how to pronounce it. Ah, but we have clues.

First, however, we need to get back to the early biblical manuscripts. Hundreds of years before the invention of paper, ancients wrote the Old Testament on animal skins, and later, papyrus. To conserve space, they printed only consonants (no vowels) in all capital letters and left no spaces between words.

To make it worse for us, after the Jews returned from Babylon, their respect for the personal name of God intensified. They considered the name so holy that to speak it aloud would dishonor it. After the Exile in Babylon, so far as we know, no Jews ever spoke the sacred name aloud. When they came across it in the biblical texts, they substituted *Adonai* (the common name for *God* in Hebrew, which literally means, "My Great Lord").

You can spot the sacred name in English translations—which appears 6,828 times. Most versions translate it as LORD (notice the initial large capital letter, followed by small capital letters).

Here's where the situation gets more difficult. The sacred name is written with four consonants. If you like impressive words, theologians refer to it as the Tetragrammaton. Those four letters are YWHW. Or they could be JVJV—because of interchangeable pronunciation of those consonants.

The problem gets worse. During the Middle Ages, somebody inserted the vowels from *Adonai* between each of the consonants.

Voila! In English, they found an easy pronunciation: "Jehovah." That stuck for several hundred years.

But no longer. For the past hundred years, scholars have argued against that unjustified insertion. "Jehovah can't be correct," they assert. "It's probably more accurate to pronounce the sacred name as *Yahweh*." Today, this is the generally accepted spelling and pronunciation, although a few voices insist that it's Yahveh.

Here's something to show the influence of Yahweh in popular names. Whenever we read a name in the Old Testament that begins with *Je* or *Jo* in names such as Jeremiah or Jonathan, it's the shortened form of the sacred name.

Sacred and Personal

I've used both terms to refer to Yahweh. Why do we single that out as the most important, personal, and sacred name? The quick answer is that it's the *covenant* name of God.

A covenant is an agreement between two parties (see chapter 13). In this case, it means that God entered into an agreement for the blessing of humanity. Such an agreement sets down conditions for both parties. Usually it meant something like God saying, "If you obey these words, then I will bless you."

If the covenant name sounds a bit heavy, think of Yahweh as God's family name. This means that its proper use is limited to those who are part of God's adopted family—the Jews of the Old Testament. Christian theology, however, says followers of Jesus Christ are spiritual Jews; consequently, Christians feel entitled to use the sacred name. Like the word *mother* or *father*, it's a name reserved only for God's children—believers—and biblical writers often refer to the Jews and to Christians as the children of God.

The name is like a sacred password. Those who belonged to the family, then, were the only ones with authorized access to the sacred name.

An Explanation of the Covenant Name

The name *Yahweh* first appears in Exodus 3:14–15. (Well, again, I need to explain. Readers can find LORD in Genesis, but scholars agree that those passages were put into written form after the Exodus experience.)

To set up the story, Moses, raised in the courts of Egypt, fled into the country of Midian. He became a shepherd. Forty years later, he was with his sheep and spotted a strange sight: A bush was aflame. There was something strange about that. Although he saw the roaring fire, nothing was happening to the bush—it simply didn't burn up.

When Moses moved closer to investigate, he heard a voice telling him to take off his sandals. He was standing on holy ground, the voice said.

Moses listened to all the things the voice said. It was God who commanded Moses to return to Egypt to see Pharaoh. God wanted the king to free the Jews, because it was time for them to go into the land promised to Abraham and his descendants. The Jews had lived in Egypt for more than four hundred years, most of that time as slaves. Among other tasks, they built the pyramids and the sphinx.

It was now emancipation time.

There was just one problem: Moses wasn't sure he wanted to take on that commission. The shepherd looked at himself and his limited abilities. He realized the danger and the audacity of what God had commanded. Moses asked, "Uh, but, who shall I say sent me?"

"YHWH" is the word he hears.

That's the answer, but it's not that simple. The answer continues to trouble translators. They don't know how to convey that reply in a word or a phrase. One way they've done it is to put the translation in all caps so that it reads "I AM WHO I AM." However, that doesn't quite translate the meaning.

Some have suggested that it should read, "I am what (or who) I will be." Unfortunately for us, that doesn't make it much clearer. Perhaps it's better to think of the answer intending to mean, "I am the one who always was, is now, and ever will be."

The translators agree on one thing: The name God uses comes from the word meaning "to be."

Today, most Christians use Yahweh (although a few cling to Jehovah), but the attitude is that Jesus taught a more familiar pathway to God and that it's not desecrating to the sacredness or holiness of God to speak in personal terms.

What's in a Name?

So what's the big deal about that sacred name? Moses hesitated in following the command from God. Back in Egypt, as soon as he began to speak, Pharaoh or someone else would challenge, "Who sent you? What's his name?"

Let's go backward again. This story of Moses meeting God presupposes a background of polytheism—a time when people worshiped and placated many gods. Unless they knew a god's name, it was impossible to enter into a relationship or to worship. How could they know who they were obeying or serving?

Yet it's more than that. Today, we use names as convenient labels to differentiate one person from another. In the ancient world, to ask for a person's name held a more serious meaning. Names expressed an individual's character—the person's very self.

To use a person's name meant to *know* who that person really was. Two examples in the Old Testament may make this clear. After Joshua led the people across the Jordan River and into the Promised Land, a man named Achan sinned. The name *Achan* means "trouble." When the man is punished for his wrongdoing, Joshua asks *Achan*

[Trouble], "Why did you bring trouble on us? The LORD is bringing trouble on you today" (Josh. 7:25 NRSV).

Nabal (lit. "fool") refused to help David when he fled from King Saul. The man's wife says to David, "May my lord pay no attention to that wicked man Nabal. He is just like his name—his name is Fool, and folly goes with him" (1 Sam. 25:25).

These two examples show us the importance of names—an expression of character. It's a way to define who someone is.

The idea of a name also carries a more subtle idea. Not only do we know who people are by their names, but it also means we have some power over them. In the New Testament, Jesus encountered a man possessed by evil spirits and he asked, "What is your name?" (Mark 5:9).

The man answered, "Legion" (figuratively meaning a multitude), and then Jesus cast out the evil spirits. People believed that if they knew the name, they could free the person from demonic power.

If people knew gods' names, it implied that they could placate them and receive what they wanted. Many ancient religions had elaborate rituals or sacrifices to satisfy the gods that brought needed rain and fruitfulness to their crops. By knowing their gods' names, they could ask for divine intervention in times of trouble.

Another aspect of knowing the name implies a relationship. After Yahweh's self-revelation, Moses explained God to the Israelites. From then on, they no longer worshiped a vague, undefined deity, but one they could approach and talk to, someone they knew by observing the way God acted.

My family and I saw this clearly during the nearly six years we lived in Kenya, East Africa. Africans carefully watched white-skinned people and gave them names that emphasized their character. We worked among the Luo people in a then-primitive area. They named our son *Gore-oko,* which means "a risk taker," someone who will try anything. Unlike many white children, along with his African friends, our son ate insects and birds (which we didn't know about until later).

They gave me two names: *Omore* ("a happy person") and *Haraka* ("fast or quick"). By naming us, the Africans had entered into a relationship with us. That is, they knew how to approach us because they knew some of our essential qualities.

That's why God's name—especially Yahweh—is important. By self-revealing the sacred name, God enters into a covenant. That is, the divine one was saying to the people of Israel, "You now have a claim on my divine power because you know me."

God's self-revelation is concentrated in the name Yahweh. That divine name not only reveals God's nature, but it also implies authority, holiness, and other divine characteristics.

That implication helps to explain the great reverence for the name among the Jews. The reverence is also based on the third of the Ten Commandments: "You shall not misuse the name of the LORD your God, for the LORD will not hold anyone guiltless who misuses his name" (Exod. 20:7).

Here are examples of the right use of Yahweh in the Old Testament:

- Prophets gave messages, citing the sacred name as their authority (Deut. 18:19; Jer. 26:20).
- Moses pronounced blessings and cursings in that name; the people considered them as potent and certain (see Num. 23–24).
- Oaths taken and sworn to by Yahweh's name are binding (Deut. 6:13).
- Battles fought in that name assure victory (Ps. 20:7).
- People "call on the name of the LORD" (Gen. 12:8; 1 Kings 18:24), confident that it gives them personal access to God's guidance and power.
- The Bible contains warnings against blaspheming or defiling the holy name (see Lev. 18:21).

The name of Yahweh becomes a sign of the divine presence, and by implication, divine help. Other nations feared Israel because they called on the name of Yahweh (Deut. 28:10).

In short, those who know the name of God (Ps. 9:10) know the divine identity and personal character. They trust the God who makes promises and delivers them from their enemies.

In the New Testament, Jesus prayed, "I have revealed you to those whom you gave me out of the world. . . . I have made you known to them, and will continue to make you known in order that the love you have for me may be in them" (John 17:6, 26). Jesus' words say that his mission on earth was to reveal the purpose and character of God.

Yahweh, the Covenant Name

We can't separate the disclosure of God's name from human experience. Beginning with Moses learning the name of Yahweh, the people began to perceive who God is—the one who rescued them from Egyptian bondage, led them into the Promised Land, and guided their daily lives.

From then on, the name of Yahweh was sometimes combined with other names to give a stronger picture of the divine nature. Here are the important ones.

1. The most notable cognate is *Yahweh Sabaoth* (or *tsebaoth*), often translated as "Lord of Hosts," which occurs 279 times in the Old Testament. Sabaoth comes from a Hebrew word that means "hosts" (or "armies") and came to refer to heavenly warriors engaged in a holy war against cults or against disobedience to God.

2. *Yahweh Elohe Israel.* The Hebrew name means "LORD-God of Israel," and it appears in the writings of Isaiah, Jeremiah, and Psalms. Other similar names are *Netsah Israel,* "the Glory of Israel" (1 Sam. 15:29), and *Abir Yisrael,* "the Mighty One of Israel" (Isa. 1:24).

3. *Yahweh-yireh.* This means "the LORD will provide." It occurs in Genesis 22:14, commemorating the provision of the ram in place of Isaac for Abraham's sacrifice on Mount Moriah.

4. *Yahweh-nissi.* This name means "the LORD is my Banner," in honor of God's defeat of the Amalekites (Exod. 17:15), which was Israel's first battle after leaving Egypt.

5. *Yahweh-shalom.* This phrase means "the LORD is Peace," the name Gideon called the altar that he built in Ophrah (Judg. 6:24).

6. *Yahweh-shammah*. This name expresses the truth that "THE LORD IS THERE," referring to the city that the prophet Ezekiel saw in a vision (Ezek. 48:35).

CHAPTER 3

God's Other Names

The Bible has a variety of ways of referring to God. With each name, the writer points to a different aspect of the divine personality. Unfortunately for English readers, this doesn't always come through in our translations.

Someone has said that we can't name God and yet we have many names for God. These names come to us through the Bible as ways to help us understand the divine nature. Yet they are obscure enough that none of them ever gives us the perfect focus on God.

When the Bible speaks of the "name," it stands for the revelation of God in relationship to human beings. In ancient cultures, people didn't use a person's name just to distinguish one individual from another as we do today. The name partially defined or explained a person. We see this in nicknames such as "Red," "Pee Wee," or "Slim." Each of them partially describes, but no name ever fully describes anyone.

Whenever we talk about the name (or names) of God in the Bible, it helps if we focus on self-revelation—that God chose to be known by us. Any time we encounter one of the names, it's there to explain to us about the way God operates in human lives.

During my seminary days, a professor used to speak of the Incomprehensible One—to make it clear to us that no matter how much we knew or understood (or thought we did), we still had not grasped the nature of God.

One way to categorize the names of God is to divide them into groups: (1) the covenant name of Yahweh (see chapter 2) and (2) the general names of God used in the Bible.

El and *Elohim* want us to grasp the idea of God as the exalted one—that God is strong, mighty, and one to be held in awe.

El, the general word for God, occurs 238 times in the Old Testament. El was already the common name for deity in ancient Middle East cultures. When it appears in the Bible, it can refer to the God of Israel or to a Canaanite god, such as Baal. It carries with it the idea of strength.

The plural form, *Elohim*, occurs more than two thousand times and refers to the God of creation or the God who provides. It also means the supreme ruler.

In the Bible, El often has a qualifier such as in Deuteronomy 5:9: "For I, the LORD [Yahweh] your God [El], am a jealous God [El]."

Here are other names compounded to El:

- *El Shaddai*, "God, the One Dwelling in the Mountains" appears forty-seven times (thirty-one of them in the Book of Job) as the name of God worshiped by Abraham, Isaac, and Jacob and commonly used until the time of Moses. Some English versions translate this as "God Almighty" (see Gen. 17:1 NRSV).

- *El Elyon,* "Most High" or "Exalted One," appears only thirty-one times in the Old Testament. In Genesis 14, Melchizedek is a priest of El Elyon, and he blesses Abraham. It's a general word for God, although in some places, it's used as a synonym for Yahweh (see Deut. 32:8–9).
- *El Olam,* "the Everlasting One" or "God of Eternity," was a word borrowed from the Canaanite god of Beer-sheba and was used to mean Yahweh, the everlasting God.
- *El Berith,* the "God of the Covenant," appears in Judges 9:46.
- *El Roi,* "the God who sees me," was a name used by Hagar in the desert (Gen. 16:13).
- *El Elohe-Israel,* was used from the time of Joshua. It means "the God of Israel." It showed the relationship of the twelve tribes to God, as in Joshua 8:30.

Elohim, although the plural of El, is usually translated in the singular. *The plural name?* Does that mean more than one God? The scholars insist it's an intensified form for the supreme God, or the plural of majesty, somewhat in the way Queen Victoria supposedly once said, "We are not amused," when she referred only to herself.

That explanation makes sense, especially because the Old Testament repeatedly states there is only one God.

Eloah appears only fifty-seven times, and all but sixteen of them are in the Book of Job. Some think that because

Job and his three "comforting" friends aren't identified as Israelites, the poet may have used the generic word for God to avoid the specific concepts associated with the Hebrew terms such as Lord (Yahweh).

Adonai is more a title than a name. One scholar refers to it as "the social title" for God. Adonai means "my Great Lord," and it's the plural of majesty from Adon ("Lord"). People also used the word as a title of respect for social superiors such as subjects to kings, slaves to their owners, or wives to their husbands. This is the word that post-exilic Jews substituted for Yahweh when reading the Old Testament scrolls aloud.

Many names of God are compounds of Yahweh, as shown in chapter 2, such as Yahweh-Nissi and God our Banner (Exod. 17:15–16). Part of the way we understand God is by comparison. By using terms familiar with their culture, people in biblical times had a stronger picture of God's character and activity.

Imagine what it must have been like for a person in ancient Canaan to gaze at the huge, immovable rocks. It could immediately bring to mind the strength and permanence of God. Therefore, it makes sense for the biblical writers to refer to God as the *Rock*, as in Isaiah 30:29. The term also appears several times in the poetic writings.

Here are other names and images used of God in the Bible:

- *Abba*. Abba is an Aramaic word much like our "daddy" or "papa." It occurs three times. Jesus used it in prayer shortly before his crucifixion (Mark 14:36).

- *Branch of Righteousness.* Used by Jeremiah, this name refers to the coming messianic figure who will reign as king to execute judgment and righteousness in the earth (see Jer. 23:5–6). Christians often interpret this as a prophecy about Jesus Christ becoming a human to serve as the righteous king.
- *Father.* This name explains the familial relationship to all who belong to God (Matt. 5:16; 28:19).
- *Judge.* This is the one who settles disputes and metes out justice and is called the judge of all the earth in Genesis 18:25.
- *King.* God was the original and only king of Israel and of all peoples. The king of Israel was to be a representative of God's presence among the people.
- *Servant,* a term in the writings of Isaiah, identifies the divine person who will save Israel. The servant is holy, just, and righteous and will bring Israel back to God so that they may become a light to other nations. (Christians generally apply the servant passages to Jesus.)
- *Shepherd.* The Jews easily envisioned a shepherd who gently led his flock, fed them, and gathered lambs in his arms, as shown in Isaiah 40:11 and Jeremiah 31:10.
- *Wisdom.* Wisdom speaks in Proverbs 8:1–36 as the one who always says and does what is righteous. The language makes wisdom equal to Yahweh (Col. 1:13–2:3).
- *Word of God.* In the New Testament, this clearly refers to Jesus Christ (John 1:1, 14).

CHAPTER 4

Where in the World Is God?

Where *is* God? OK, you may think it's a trick question because, as a child, you learned that God is everywhere. That's true. But where, *specifically*, is God? Where's the place or sphere of the divine one's operations?

Here's one way of getting to the question. First, God is everywhere at all times and in all places. This leads us to ask, But how does God operate in human lives?

To answer that, theologians have argued for centuries and continue to debate between the God-up-there and the God-within-us. Or the God far away and the nearby God. Or we can sound erudite and ask, "Which position do you advocate?" God's transcendence ("up there") or God's immanence ("with us")?

No matter which they opt for, theologians agree that Yahweh is both, but they tend to emphasize one or the other.

The point of the question isn't whether God is far away or within us. This is why the question is important. Somewhere in shaping our own belief system, we have tended to hang heavy on one side or the other. Our prejudice (and it is that) also enables us to understand how we behave in daily living—such as how we pray or how we address problems that confront us.

When we pray, for instance, do we address primarily "Our Father, who art in heaven . . . hear me"? That's God far away. Or do we pray, "Abba, Father, you're with me and know my thoughts"? Most of us shift between these points, but we probably emphasize one or the other.

Before I explain the difference, bear in mind that faithful followers of God stand on both sides of the issue.

Transcendence

This word carries two meanings. First, it's a way of saying that God is different from humanity. Some people refer to the "otherness" of the Holy One, but they mean that God just isn't the same as we are.

Second, it speaks of the remoteness or distance between God and humanity. In primitive days when people thought of the universe like a three-story structure, that was important. They understood that heaven was above, the earth was in the middle, and hell was below the ground—literally. To them, God sat on the remotest clouds in the heavens and stared down at us but remained detached and far away.

God's transcendence is emphasized in such biblical statements as "King eternal, immortal, invisible, the only God" (1 Tim. 1:17). Or the "blessed and only Ruler, the King of kings and Lord of lords, who alone is immortal and who lives in unapproachable light, whom no one has seen or can see" (1 Tim. 6:15–16a).

Transcendence says God's nature and being are so far removed from us that we can't possibly understand the God who is Spirit and beyond our senses. God is external of the world and creatures as the sovereign creator and judge of the world.

Immanence

When we speak of immanence, we refer to the idea of God being with us. God is still different from humanity but not remote or far away. God is near us. With us. Around us. This is the one who says, "I have loved you with an everlasting love" or "I will never leave you."

This is the idea of intimacy. Many Christians speak of the indwelling God, the Holy Spirit within us. When Jesus prayed in the garden before his arrest, it was an intimate prayer of a man in agony. Psalm 23 comes from someone who experienced the closeness of God. "Even though I walk through the valley of the shadow of death, I will fear no evil, for you are with me" (Ps. 23:4).

This focus on immanence reminds believers of Jesus, who was God, who came to earth and was born a human. Jesus "had to be made like his brothers in every way. . . . Because he himself suffered when he was tempted, he is able to help those who are being tempted" (Heb. 2:17–18).

Why Is This Question Important?

For most of us today, this isn't a serious issue, but it's a question that thinkers of the past discussed and even argued over. It's not really an issue of whether God is transcendent or immanent, but the heart of it comes down to this: Can we know God?

If God is totally "out there," it puts the Holy One beyond human ability to tap into knowing, understanding, and experiencing the divine being. Our minds can't know anything beyond and behind natural phenomenon. Therefore, the reasoning goes, we must be ignorant of divine things. This is basically the position of agnostics—the ones who don't deny, but shrug and say, "I simply don't know."

Because we know or perceive only through our senses and faculties, they say, how can we know that which is beyond both?

The other danger is pantheism—God is in and part of everything. This means God is present in everything from stalks of corn to mountain summits. God is so identified with the world that the next step is for people to say—and there are those who embrace New Age teaching who do— "I am god. You are god." The Bible contains no support for such thinking.

Now I'll expose my prejudice. I begin by referring to the immense distance of time, space, and divine character that distinguishes the Creator from us, the creation. Nature can teach us, but it can't put us in a relationship with our Creator. The Bible makes it clear that by our searching, studying, thinking, or reasoning alone, we won't know God. By ourselves, we can't step into God's world.

Now here's the good news. We *can* know God—but only because God chooses to reveal himself. God takes the initiative by breaking into our world and bridging the gap. When God reveals himself, it makes us more conscious of the distance of that separation. "Oh, that I might find God" is then the human cry.

The self-revealing aspect of Yahweh implies that God has chosen to be in relationship with us. If we have no way to reach high enough (or to think lofty enough thoughts) to perceive a God who is greater than our thoughts, the relationship can come in only one way—God breaks into our world.

Yahweh is above and beyond the historic world of time and space. At the same time, God visits the world and makes that personal presence known—obviously not to everyone, but certainly to Israel and those with open hearts.

When we read Genesis 1, for example, we see the picture of the God-beyond-human-existence. This is the Creator who speaks and the world comes into existence. Immediately water appears, fish swim, and flowers grow. This is God-up-there, the transcendent God.

Genesis 2 and 3 repeat some of the creation account but with a different emphasis. This time we glimpse the immanent side. The divine one walks with Adam in the garden and gives permission for the man to name the animals. This is the Creator who, aware of the creature's loneliness, creates a companion.

For another example, think of the Israelites in the wilderness. God had the people build a tent—called the tabernacle—as the center of their worship. Within the innermost part of that tent, they placed the ark of the covenant, which is a box that signified his presence. That ark symbolically assured Israel of God's presence with them.

Once they finished the tabernacle, the God-up-there came down from heaven in a cloud and filled the tent.

What a powerful object lesson for them: The tent symbolized the "holy distance" from the chosen people; the ark inside the tabernacle signified God's abiding presence. They had the opportunity to grasp both aspects at the same time—Yahweh coming down to them and Yahweh being with them.

In the New Testament, we learn of God in Jesus Christ, who "is the image of the invisible God" (Col. 1:15), the one who is the "radiance of God's glory and the exact representation of his being" (Heb. 1:3). This is Emmanuel—God with us—the immanent one (see Matt. 1:23). "Anyone who has seen me has seen the Father," Jesus said (John 14:9).

The Blend for Us

We find a harmony between transcendence and immanence all through the New Testament. Heaven is the throne, and God controls all earthly powers. Yet the loving Creator exercises vigilant care over all creation. The Holy One clothes the flowers, feeds the birds, and not even a sparrow falls without God's knowledge (Matt. 6:30).

This God is knowable.

CHAPTER 5

Examining God's Character

——————— ∞ ———————

Who is God?

What is God like—really like?

The Old Testament doesn't define God, and yet the writers show a deep understanding of Yahweh's nature. Instead of trying to fit God into an academic formula, they pointed to him in action. It's as if they respond with, "You want to understand God? OK, look at God's actions. The actions explain the divine character."

The systematic theologians like to tidy it up for us—after all, that's why they are called *systematic*. They love making statements, such as "there are five things that define the character of our Creator." The Bible doesn't categorize God quite so neatly. I do, however, bow to them in trying to explain God. For centuries, systematic theologians have wrestled with defining God's nature.

Let's consider first the incommunicable attributes of God. Every theology book I know has a chapter on the attributes of God—which is the same thing as defining God's character. Incommunicable attributes are characteristics we human beings don't have because they belong only to God. The serious thinkers emphasized the absolute distinction or separation between God and humanity. Most of these attributes seem rather obvious, but here are the major ones.

Self-Existence

The scholars sometimes speak of the independence of God. They mean that God doesn't need anything outside of the divine self. God remains totally independent of all creatures. In fact, all creatures depend on God to exist. Psalm 115:3 says it this way: "Our God is in heaven; he does whatever pleases him."

In an earlier chapter I wrote about God's most important name—Yahweh—and that name embodies this idea. This is as if God steps into human lives and says, "If you obey me, I'll be your God."

Omnipresence

God is not only present everywhere at the same time, but Yahweh is actively involved in every part of creation. God didn't design the world, get events moving, and then abandon it. The Bible teaches God's moment-by-moment concern for all people everywhere.

A friend once said it to me this way: "It's not so much that God is everywhere as that God is the everywhere itself."

Immutability

This is another tongue twister the learned theologians love to throw around. It's a big word to express the idea that God doesn't change. Here's the way I learned it in seminary: "God is forever unchangeable in character or attributes and also with divine purposes and promises."

Or how about this? "But the plans of the LORD stand firm forever, the purposes of his heart through all generations" (Ps. 33:11).

Immutability, at its simplest, means that God speaks and it happens. The divine one never makes mistakes or errors of judgment. God is forever the same in divine being and perfection, as well as in purposes and promises. Sounds obvious, doesn't it?

Oops, but what about the places in the Old Testament that say God repents or changes?

To prepare for the answer, here's a firm principle about God's immutability: "God is not a man, that he should lie, nor a son of man, that he should change his mind. Does he speak and then not act? Does he promise and not fulfill?" (Num. 23:19).

Let's look at two instances of God's mind-changing action. In the story of the Jews worshiping the golden calf, Yahweh told Moses that the people had turned away and were "a stiff-necked people." Then he said, "Now leave me alone so that my anger may burn against them and that I may destroy them. Then I will make you into a great nation" (Exod. 32:10).

Moses begged God not to destroy the people. The Bible reads, "Then the LORD relented [older versions used *repented*] and did not bring on his people the disaster he had threatened" (v. 14).

Here's the second example. In the Book of Jonah, God told the prophet to go to the people of Nineveh and pronounce judgment and destruction because of their wickedness. After the Ninevites heard the message of Jonah that they would die in forty days, they repented and turned from their wicked ways. "When God saw what they did and how they turned from their evil ways, he had compassion and did not bring upon them the destruction he had threatened" (Jon. 3:10).

Because they changed, God didn't wipe them out. It would seem on the surface that if we beg God, we can change the divinely determined course of history.

Is there a contradiction in the Bible?

Of course not. These verses mean that, *from the human viewpoint,* it seems as if God changes. In both instances, God promised destruction based on the people's continued evil doings. If we accept those words as threats or warnings rather than pronouncements, it helps us understand. The purpose of Yahweh's words was to get the wicked to put away their evil doings. If they turned and followed God, the destruction wouldn't happen. If they continued in the same way, the punishment would come.

Think of it this way. God's loving nature wants humanity to have only the best. If we obey, we get the blessings. If we refuse to follow, we pay the price for our disobedience.

Infinity

This word tells us that God isn't subject to limitations. Those who originally used the term were trying to remind us that God is limitless—not a mere endless continuum as we use the word today.

God is absolutely perfect. How can we possibly understand—let alone explain—perfection? God is a being who is free from limitations and boundaries. For instance, when we speak of his boundless love, we're not talking about the quantity of love but a love that is free of all limitations and defects. God is absolute perfection and unlimited in knowledge, wisdom, goodness, love, righteousness, holiness, and all other qualities. "Great is the LORD and most worthy of praise; his greatness no one can fathom" (Ps. 145:3).

In relation to time, we think of God's eternity. Scripture usually represents this as endless duration, meaning that God is above time and therefore not subject to its limitations. For Yahweh, there is only the eternal present and no past or future. When we think of God and space, we call it God's immensity—everywhere present, filling every point in space, but in no way bounded by space.

This is the beginning. In the next chapters, we'll look more closely at the being and personality of God.

CHAPTER 6

God's Morals

———————— ∞ ————————

In some ways, we are like God. At our best, we have qualities or attributes that dimly reflect God's.

That which we see and acknowledge in other humans is only a limited and imperfect reflection of the infinitely unlimited and perfect one. We call these the communicable attributes of God. Here are the major qualities.

Goodness

God is perfectly holy, but that's not what the term means. This part of God's being reveals itself by doing good for others. That perfection prompts Yahweh to deal kindly and bountifully with all creatures. The Bible refers to it repeatedly, such as the words of Jesus: "He [God] causes his sun to rise on the evil and the good, and sends rain on the righteous and the unrighteous" (Matt. 5:45).

Holiness

"The Holy One of Israel" is a common Old Testament term, and it means that no evil resides in God's character.

The divine nature opposes sin and all wrongdoing. Isaiah saw a vision of heavenly beings that cried out, "Holy, holy, holy is the LORD Almighty" (Isa. 6:3).

The underlying thought of holiness is being separate from all that's impure. This is the divine perfection by which God is absolutely distinct from all creatures and exalted above them in infinite majesty. God is free from all moral impurity or sin and, thus, is morally perfect. By our obedience he declares us holy—people separated for God. The term *saints* comes from the same root—people who are set aside for divine purposes.

Justice

God is the one who eventually makes all things right. Although the justness of God's character has been ignored, many people today are crying out to make our world equitable. We don't always see fairness and impartiality, but the Bible assures that one day God will bring ultimate justice into our world.

The justice of God manifests itself by giving rewards or blessings, often called remunerative justice. That which reveals itself in meting out punishment is known as retributive justice. The former is an expression of love and the latter of wrath. Our sense of making things right, our cries for justice, reflect this divine virtue.

Knowledge

In my seminary days, I copied a definition of God's knowledge on the flyleaf of one my textbooks: "God in a manner all his own, knows himself and all things possible and actual." That sentence means that there's nothing God doesn't know.

The Creator embodies all knowledge and doesn't obtain it from learning, observing, or experience, but he himself is the source. This knowledge is complete and always present in the mind of the Creator. We call that omniscience, because God knows all things—past, present, and future.

We know a few things of the past, we live in the present, and we have some sense of things future. As one of my friends said, "God lays time out on a flat line and can see the past as fully as the future. Nothing is unknown." God says, "I make known the end from the beginning, from ancient times, what is still to come" (Isa. 46:10).

Love

As the most quoted verse in the Bible, John 3:16 asserts that God loved the world—every person ever born. That verse, as well as others, points out this great quality of God. All creation as well as our own existence and redemption are the results of love. Even when humans rebel, God's love never diminishes. In fact, Paul says it this way: "But God demonstrates his own love for us in this: While we were still sinners, Christ died for us" (Rom. 5:8). This is love in action, love proven.

The unmerited love of God reveals itself in pardoning sin. We call this grace. The love that relieves the misery of those who are bearing the consequences of sin is called mercy or compassion. When love bears with the sinners who don't heed instructions and warnings of God, it is called longsuffering or forbearance.

Power

This is what we often label "omnipotence." It refers to God's limitless power. Jesus himself said, "All things are possible with God" (Mark 10:27). Obviously this doesn't extend to anything self-contradictory or immoral.

That shows the difference between divine and human power. We can do many things; we can also use that ability to do evil, to oppress, to murder, or to assassinate someone's character. God's power is limited to doing good.

Righteousness

God always obeys all moral laws, such as the Ten Commandments, and asks humans to follow them as well. Righteousness means that God always does the right thing. For us, righteousness is to do the right thing at the right time. Yet it is only a shadow of what the word means when applied to God's eternal and essential righteousness.

Truth

The God of truth always represents everything exactly as it is—never misleads—and never deceives. This also means that God's plans are always honorable and true to the divine nature. God wouldn't lie; God can't lie. This is quite a contrast from earthly creatures.

Wisdom

God knows all the facts, and he has perfect understanding to make correct and equitable decisions every time. We call this *omniscience*. God always has all knowledge of every possibility and potential event.

"Oh, the depth of the riches of the wisdom and knowledge of God! How unsearchable his judgments, and his paths beyond tracing out!" (Rom. 11:33).

∞

When we think about the morals and qualities of God, it's also a message to those who believe. God's plan isn't primarily to make us happy or to enable us to enjoy life. His purpose for us is stated in Romans 8:28–29: "And we know that in all things God works for the good of those who love him, who have been called according to his purpose . . . to be conformed to the likeness of his Son."

CHAPTER 7

Personal Expressions of God

God is one, and yet God is three.

I don't know anyone who understands that statement.

Ultimately, Christians look at what the Bible says, and they believe it even if they can't comprehend it.

The Oneness of God causes no problem. It's the three-ness or the Trinity that stumbles us. The word *Trinity* never appears in the Bible. Many call the word "Christian revelation" and others say it's simply a matter of logic and analysis. Even so, it remains one of the most difficult doctrines to explain.

The concept of the Trinity means that while we want to insist, along with Judaism, that God is one, we also want to say that Yahweh exists in three persons.

As soon as we use the word *persons,* however, we're already running into trouble. So we quickly add that we don't mean persons in the usual sense of the word but rather modes or forms. That is, God expresses himself in three ways—as Father, Son, and Holy Spirit—and each possesses the whole of the divine essence.

Are you confused now?

The doctrine of the Trinity came about like this. In the second century after the resurrection of Jesus, a theologian named Tertullian (A.D. 145–220) came up with a way to explain God, which he called the Trinity. If not the originator of the term, he was the first to use it in writing. Some preferred tri-unity or three-in-one, but that's essentially a matter of word play.

Today we accept the doctrine without question—that is without questioning whether it's true. Historically, it was one of the great debates of the early church—one that went on for a couple of centuries.

In A.D. 325 at the Council of Nicea, the great theologians met and hammered out the first official statements of right belief. They condemned the teachings of a man named Sabellius. Concerned that people would recognize three separate Gods, Sabellius taught that in reality there was no distinction of personality within the Godhead. He asserted that the three names in the New Testament—Father, Son, and Holy Spirit—were designations for three *manifestations* of the one God—each temporarily used for the purpose of accomplishing salvation for humanity.

Arius, who began with the Sabellian teachings, moved on to argue that God is one. Period. He placed so much emphasis on the one-ness that Jesus Christ the Son and the Holy Spirit became subordinate beings whom the Father "willed into existence" to act as divine agents in dealing with the world. Above I wrote, "Each possesses the whole of the divine essence." Arius wouldn't acknowledge the truth of such a statement.

Today, a minority of those who call themselves Christians don't accept the Trinity and refer to themselves as the oneness people or sometimes as "Jesus Only." Consequently, they don't baptize in the name of the triune God. One of their big arguments is that when we reach heaven, we'll see only one God. Who we'll see, they say, is Jesus. That's the modern version of Arius.

Historically, the theological leaders of the church declared the Trinity the valid description of God. As if that ended it! Now we have to try to explain something that defies explanation.

I think of their functions to make the term *Trinity* make sense. All three—Father, Son, and Holy Spirit—are the object of prayer and adoration. The Bible lists all three as involved in the activities of creation and salvation. The monotheism or one-God concept of the Old Testament is maintained in the New Testament.

Three categories of the New Testament texts show the way this doctrine progressed. First came the revelation of the unity of the Father and the Son. Such verses deal with what theologians call the *incarnation*—Jesus laying aside the divine nature and being born as a human being. Many texts show a close relationship between Jesus and God (Rom. 8:31–34; 1 Cor. 11:3; 15:20–28; Col. 2:9; 1 John 5:20).

Second, a number of places speak of a similarly close relationship between Jesus and the Holy Spirit. In the Old Testament, the Holy Spirit (or the Spirit of God) is understood as the agency of God's power and presence with individuals and communities. In the New Testament, Jesus uniquely receives the Holy Spirit at his baptism

(Luke 3:22). He then becomes the mediator of the activity of the Spirit (Acts 2:33 and elsewhere) and is identified with the Spirit in places such as Romans 8:26–27, 34 and John 14. The Bible also has expressions such as "the Spirit of the Lord" and "the Spirit of Jesus." Galatians 4:6 says that God sends "the Spirit of his Son."

In the New Testament, the Holy Spirit becomes an active presence beginning with Acts 2. After that, the references to the Holy Spirit mean the presence and the activity of God and of Jesus Christ.

Third, there are passages in which all three persons of the Trinity are mentioned in the same context, as I've shown below. I especially point out the baptismal formula of Matthew 28:19.

Fourth, a variety of biblical examples of the Trinity exist, so it wasn't just a clever idea that Tertullian pulled out of creative imagination. In the Old Testament, repeatedly the plural form for God, *Elohim,* is used about two thousand times with a singular verb. This hints of a plurality of persons within the Godhead, which is and always has been regarded as one. Deuteronomy 6:4 has long been known as the *Shema* [lit. "hear"] or the rallying point of Judaism: "Hear, O Israel: the LORD our God, the LORD is One." This affirms the unity of God.

This was especially important in the early days of Israel. They were a people who lived among idol worshipers. Their neighbors bowed to a plurality of gods. The clear Old Testament message is that God is one. This powerful statement finds itself repeated through the inspired messages of the prophets.

Here are two instances of the plural form of the Godhead:

- "Let us make man in our image, in our likeness" (Gen. 1:26).
- "Come, let us [God] go down and confuse their language" (Gen. 11:7).

In the New Testament, we find a number of instances where all three members of the Trinity are mentioned:

- When Jesus came out of the water after being baptized by John the Baptist: "At that moment heaven was opened, and he saw the Spirit of God descending like a dove and lighting on him. And a voice from heaven said, 'This is my Son, whom I love'" (Matt. 3:16–17).
- Paul's oft-quoted benediction reads, "May the grace of the Lord Jesus Christ, and the love of God, and the fellowship of the Holy Spirit be with you all" (2 Cor. 13:14).
- Peter states that we were chosen by God the Father, sanctified (or set apart) by the work of the Spirit, because of the death of Jesus Christ (1 Pet. 1:2).

The relationship of Father and Son in the New Testament is prominent. Jesus became human and continually relied on the Father during his earthly ministry. The Holy Spirit was in the background until introduced by Jesus (John 14–16).

I have no trouble believing in the Trinity. Most of those who struggle to make the term meaningful resort to comparisons and metaphors, such as:

- C. S. Lewis described the Trinity as a cube with six squares while remaining one body.

- Frederick Buechner compared the Trinity to looking into a mirror. We see the interior self known only to the looker, the visible face known to others, and the invisible power to communicate our interior selves so that people will know the real us.
- Others have spoken of the sun, its rays, and its warmth.
- A popular explanation is to think of three strands in a rope.

Not being able to explain the term doesn't make the Trinity less real. I can name many things in this life that I accept, but I wouldn't know how to speak the first sentence of explanation.

One of the greatest theologians of the church, Augustine, said that without the Trinity there could be no fellowship or love in God, and that the divine tri-unity involved an interrelationship in which the divine perfections find eternal expression independent of the creation of the world and humanity.

For me, the simplest way to get this teaching clear is to see how each part of the Godhead functions.

God the Father

The term *Father* is frequently applied to God as the Creator as well as the Father of Israel (Deut. 32:6). In the New Testament, the word also refers to God to express the family relationship of all believers as children and God as the parent. In a deeper sense, however, the term applies to the first person of the Trinity to express a relationship to the second person, Jesus Christ. God the Father's love and compassion planned for our salvation.

Jesus Christ the Son

The second person is called "Son" or "Son of God" and bears the name not only as the "One and Only" Son (John 1:14), but also as the Messiah or Christ, chosen of God. Jesus is described in the New Testament as having a special birth brought about by the work of the Holy Spirit. Jesus sacrificed himself for our salvation (Eph. 1:3–14).

The Holy Spirit

Many, especially outside the church, speak of the Spirit as a higher power or an important influence. The Spirit, however, clearly stands out in the Bible as a person (see John 14:16).

The New Testament speaks of the Spirit in a variety of ways. The Spirit:
- knows everything and teaches believers (John 14:26),
- can be grieved (Isa. 63:10; Eph. 4:30),
- helps believers pray (Rom. 8:26–27),
- guides believers (Acts 16:7–10), and
- gives believers gifts and abilities (1 Cor. 12:7–11).

The New Testament also speaks of the work of the Holy Spirit as speaking, searching, bearing witness, commanding, revealing, striving, and interceding. The Holy Spirit applies or brings us salvation.

∞

The concept of the Trinity isn't an explanation but a definition of the being and activities of God. No matter how much we know, the Trinity remains something we can never explain, but we can believe. Nearly a thousand years ago Thomas Aquinas said that God is intelligible but incomprehensible.

When I was a new convert, I asked pastor Walter Olsen to help me understand the Trinity. He never fully succeeded, of course, but in our discussions he made a statement about the relationship within the Trinity that has stayed with me: "Characteristic of the triune family is their selfless love for one another. There's no vying for leadership, no jealousy, and no infighting. Each esteems and defers to the other in a way that makes the family of the Trinity a model for all families of believers."

That was worth writing down and remembering.

CHAPTER 8

The One and Only

The New Testament is the only substantial first-century source of information about the life of Jesus. He is hardly mentioned in Jewish or Roman literature of that time.

The four Gospels provide our primary sources of information about Jesus. They were not written as biographies, but they show us his person and work. From his birth to his thirtieth year, there is only one story about his boyhood—when he spoke with the priests in the temple. The real story of Jesus begins with his baptism, and even from then on the account of his ministry isn't exhaustive. In his Gospel, John writes that he left many things unrecorded (John 21:25).

What is recorded moves quickly through his ministry, and all four writers devote considerably more coverage to the events of the last week of Jesus' life than to anything else.

Because each writer wished to emphasize a somewhat different aspect of Jesus' person and work, the accounts vary in detail. They selected the facts that best suited their purposes and didn't always follow a chronological order.

Most authorities believe that Luke comes nearest to following the actual sequence of events.

The Bible teaches the preexistence of the second person of the Trinity before the birth of Jesus at Bethlehem. This becomes the major reason why Christians affirm their belief that Jesus Christ is both God and human.

Hebrews 1:6 states that Jesus was worshiped at God's command. Lesser spiritual beings decline to be worshiped (as in Rev. 22:8–9) because worship is to be rendered only to God.

That Jesus Christ is God, the cocreator with the Father, is made clear by passages such as Colossians 1:16 and Hebrews 1:2. Yet the Bible also teaches the humanity of Jesus, one who experienced human joys and sufferings (Luke 2:40, 52; Heb. 2:10, 18; 5:8). One factor made Jesus unique from other human beings: He was born sinless and remained without sin, as expressed in places such as Hebrews 4:15.

In some ways, this is as difficult to explain as the Trinity; however, the Bible teaches that Jesus Christ has two distinct natures but is a single person, not two persons under one skin.

Names and Titles of Jesus

The doctrine of Christ or Christology deals with the person and work of Jesus Christ. Of the many titles of Jesus found in the New Testament, five reflect something significant about his person and work (Christ, Jesus, Lord, Son of God, and Son of Man). Here is a look at some of the other titles or names given in the New Testament to the second person of the Trinity.

Alpha and Omega. These are the first and last letters of the Greek alphabet. The risen Christ declared, "I am the Alpha and the Omega, the First and the Last, the Beginning and the End" (Rev. 22:13). Calling Jesus Christ the alpha and the omega acknowledges the second person of the Trinity as Creator, Savior, and the final judge of all things.

Beginning. A title that describes Christ's existence before time began. The Gospel of John declares that Jesus was present with the Father "in the beginning" and, therefore, the Creator of all things (John 1:2–3). Christ is called "the beginning" (Col. 1:18) and "the origin of God's creation" (Rev. 3:14 NRSV).

Christ. This is the New Testament equivalent of Messiah, a Hebrew word meaning "anointed one" (cf. Acts 4:27; 10:38). This title emphasized that Jesus was divinely appointed to the task of salvation.

Holy One of God. This title was given to Jesus by Peter (John 6:69), and also, remarkably, by a demon-possessed man (Mark 1:24). In their preaching, the apostles called Jesus "the Holy and Righteous One" (Acts 3:14). This title also emphasized Jesus' positive goodness and complete dedication to doing God's will.

Jesus. The name Jesus (same root as Joshua and means "God is Savior") emphasizes his role as the Savior (Matt. 1:21).

Lord. This title was sometimes used as a polite form of address, as we would say, "sir." But after the resurrection the word acquired deeper meeting, and it's the term Paul used most frequently. A title of authority or ownership, it indicates the Son's equality with the Father (Matt. 7:22; Mark 12:36–37; Luke 2:11).

One and Only Son. Older versions of the Bible translate this title as "only begotten." John's Gospel uses that title to designate Jesus' uniqueness (John 1:14, 18; 3:16, 18; 1 John 4:9). The title comes from combining two Greek words that mean "single kind." Therefore, it means the only one of its kind, that is, unique.

Son of God. This title was given to Jesus by the heavenly voice at his baptism. This message was not meant to declare that Jesus was the second person of the Trinity. Rather, it was a messianic title, a term found in the Old Testament. When applied to Jesus, it's a way to designate him as the one who would bring fulfillment to Israel and be the Messiah.

Son of Man. More than any other title, Jesus used this of himself. In the Old Testament, people recognized it as referring to a heavenly figure—a preexistent one who would come at the end of the ages as judge and as a light to the Gentiles (Mark 14:62). Jesus sometimes used this title to refer to his authority and power, as in Mark 2:10 and Luke 12:8.

The Word. With the statement, "The Word became flesh" (John 1:14), the Gospel of John clearly describes Jesus. In the Old Testament, the Jews referred to the Ten Commandments as "The Word." This tie is just one more way that the divine nature of Jesus Christ is declared. This brings the personal presence of God to a new level—life in the human world.

Roles and Offices of Jesus

Since the time of the Reformation, one important way to understand the person and the work done by Jesus Christ has been to look at three distinctive roles fulfilled by the second person of the Trinity. This also shows Jesus embodying the three principle offices in the Old Testament.

Prophetic Office. The Old Testament depicts prophets as those who receive God's word (revelation) and pass it on to the people. They stand in God's stead. When they speak it is as if Yahweh uses their voices to communicate the message.

The Old Testament promised a great prophet who would convey God's word finally and decisively to the people. Deuteronomy 18:15 is the first clear promise of that prophet. Acts 3:22–24 proclaims Jesus as the fulfillment of those words.

Priestly Office. While Old Testament prophets represented God to the people, priests represented the people to God. This is a major role of Jesus Christ (Heb. 3:1; 4:14).

By Old Testament law, the high priests presented animal sacrifices to God every year; by grace, Jesus Christ is the eternal sacrifice. The high priest prayed and interceded for the people of God. But "because Jesus lives forever, he has a permanent priesthood . . . because he always lives to intercede for them [God's people]" (Heb. 7:24–25).

Kingly Office. Jesus Christ is the eternal king over all kings. Prophecies had a partial fulfillment at Jesus' first coming. God promised that the great king would come through the tribe of Judah and the line of David. Jesus' mother Mary was from the line of David. This promise

will reach complete fulfillment when the King of kings and
Lord of lords returns.

Other descriptive names of Jesus include:

- Brother
- Example
- Friend
- Savior
- Good Shepherd
- Great Physician
- Love
- Messiah
- Son of Mary
- Master
- Redeemer
- Rescuer
- Resurrected Christ
- Teacher

Metaphors used as names for Jesus include:

- Lamb
- Bread of Life
- Lion of Judah
- The Truth
- Morning Star
- True Vine
- The Door
- The Life
- Living Water
- Cornerstone
- The Way

CHAPTER 9

The Holy One

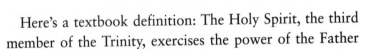

Here's a textbook definition: The Holy Spirit, the third member of the Trinity, exercises the power of the Father and the Son in creation and salvation.

In a practical way, most Christians think of the Holy Spirit as the power by which they have come to believe in Jesus Christ as their Savior.

Someone said, "Like the eyes of the body through which we see physical things, the Spirit is seldom seen directly, because that is the one through whom all else is seen in a new light." The relationship of the Father and the Son is more visible in the Gospels. It is through the eyes of the Holy Spirit that the Father-Son relationship is viewed.

This unified ministry of the Trinity shows itself like this:

- The Spirit brings the world under conviction of sin, righteousness, and judgment, and guides believers into all truth they have heard from the Father (John 12:49–50).

- The Father witnesses to and glorifies the Son (John 8:16–18, 50, 54).
- The Father and Son commission the Holy Spirit to speak in their name (John 14:16, 26).
- The Holy Spirit helps the Father and Son by helping believers (John 16:13–15).

Thus, the triune family of Father, Son, and Holy Spirit are unified in ministering to believers.

The Holy Spirit is also called Counselor or Helper (from the Greek word, *parakletos,* which means "one who speaks in favor of," such as a defense counsel). Before the crucifixion, Jesus told his disciples that he was going away, but he wouldn't leave them alone. He would send another helper, the Counselor.

The Counselor came. Believers in the early church easily grasped the concept of the Holy Spirit. Just to read the Book of Acts shows the disciples' dependence on the Spirit and the mighty acts of God taking place through the Spirit's activities. It began when Jesus' disciples prayed and waited in the upper room. Then in dramatic terms, Acts 2 tells of the sudden and powerful coming of the Holy Spirit. The Spirit "filled" them (Acts 2:4). Then and in subsequent experiences of disciples being filled, we read of mighty deeds as the gospel began with a small group of believers in Jerusalem. Each chapter tells of the expanding power of the Spirit in reaching out to bring other people to God.

The Holy Spirit fills believers, strengthens them, and assists them to fulfill the divinely appointed mission to go into the entire world. The Holy Spirit is the "other" Helper now, just as Jesus was the great helper while he lived on earth. It is through the Counselor that Father and Son abide with the disciples (John 15:26).

Descriptive names of the Holy Spirit include:

- Giver of Life
- Comforter
- Convictor of Sin
- Nourisher
- Nurturer
- Illuminator
- Transformer
- Motivator

Metaphors used as names for the Holy Spirit include:

- Breath of God
- Guarantee
- Indwelling Spirit
- Wind of God
- Wisdom

CHAPTER 10

More-than-Human God

How can we talk about God? If God is totally different from us, how can we think about God in concrete terms, let alone try to explain? If God is totally different from human creatures, then how do we find a vocabulary to speak about the mighty Creator?

When it comes to thinking about God, it may help to remember that God commanded the Israelites never to make any graven or physical image or icon to represent God, such as human form, a beast, bird, or fish. So what could they do? How did they comprehend God without some kind of visual image?

The answer—and it really seems sensible—was to use human terminology. Or another way to say it is that they used word pictures or symbols to convey what can't be expressed in human language.

The prophets and writers of the Bible turned to common terms that the people of their day would understand. For instance, when biblical writers referred to God's bodily parts such as the eyes, ears, hands, or feet, they didn't mean the words literally. Their readers—as primitive as the culture may have been—understood they wrote figuratively. Moses, Samuel, David, Daniel, and all the others used human expressions to help others understand a little of that which can't be fully comprehended any other way.

If we try to limit our explanation of Yahweh with abstract terms such as absolute being, the great unknown, or the ground of being, we lose the personalization. We have only an "it" or a "him"—and when we use such pronouns we have already moved into anthropomorphic terminology. No one has ever found a better way for people to express relationship with God.

In short, we simply can't talk about God without using human terminology.

I also believe we humans need to sense the personal aspect of God in our lives—to bring God to our level so we can understand. We identify with a loving, compassionate God when we can express the loving, compassionate portion of God's nature in terms that make sense.

The technical word to describe using human expressions to explain the beyond-human nature is *anthropomorphic*—a word not found in the Bible. It comes from two Greek words for human *(anthropos)* and form *(morphe)*. If we want to understand God, we have to come at the problem by thinking of God through using human forms or terms.

For example, after Yahweh delivered the Israelites from the Egyptians and they stopped to praise God on the other side of the Red Sea, the Song of Moses declared, "The LORD is a warrior" (Exod. 15:3). Because God had "fought" for them, this was one way of making the God of all creation understandable. Even then, the people didn't believe that God literally extended a giant arm from heaven to protect them at the Red Sea and then overthrow the Egyptians. The figure of speech expressed the truth that Yahweh intervened to save the chosen people and to destroy their oppressors.

Here are a few of the various ways biblical writers use anthropomorphic language:

- "God did not raise his hand against these leaders" (Exod. 24:11).
- "The eyes of the LORD are on the righteous" (Ps. 34:15a).
- "[The LORD's] ears are attentive to their cry" (Ps. 34:15b).
- [Jesus said], "Angels in heaven always see the face of my Father in heaven" (Matt. 18:10).
- [God said], "My heart is changed within me; all my compassion is aroused" (Hos. 11:8).
- "[The LORD's] right hand and his holy arm have worked salvation for him" (Ps. 98:1b).
- [Jesus said], "But if I drive out demons by the finger of God, then the kingdom of God has come to you" (Luke 11:20).

Judaism and Christianity aren't unique in using human terms to describe the more-than-human aspects of the divine. This kind of designation commonly appears in other ancient religions.

The Old Testament, however, goes beyond most early religions. The writers did not stop at using the body parts of God, but they also wrote of God's feelings, thoughts, and motivations. Probably more accurately, various verses might refer to the way the humans saw and understood how God thought and felt.

The human-type characteristics of Yahweh were always higher and more ethical than those of humans. By contrast, the gods of their pagan neighbors shared the same vices and were, in some sense, much like them.

For the Israelites to relate to God, they needed a divinity who would sympathize with their human feelings, understand their emotions, feel lovingly, and understand fear, anger, and worry. God didn't disappoint them.

Here are several references to Yahweh's emotions and attitudes.

- "For I, the LORD your God, am a jealous God" (Exod. 20:5).
- "Has God forgotten to be merciful? Has he in anger withheld his compassion?" (Ps. 77:9).
- "I knew that you are a gracious and compassionate God, slow to anger and abounding in love" (Jon. 4:2).
- "Great is our Lord and mighty in power; his understanding has no limit" (Ps. 147:5).
- "The LORD is compassionate and gracious, slow to anger, abounding in love" (Ps. 103:8).
- "Then the word of the LORD came to Samuel: 'I am grieved that I have made Saul king'" (1 Sam. 15:10–11).

Anthropomorphism gets support from the idea of God's self-revelation. The Bible makes it clear that we need to know who God is so that we serve, love, and worship the one who loves us. The more we understand about God, the more we can grasp divine purposes and interpret those actions of the past and present. As we comprehend God's nature through anthropomorphic terms, we move onward until we get the full impact in the incarnation—when God took on human life and form through Jesus Christ.

In the New Testament, we have fewer anthropomorphic pictures because the writers focus on the God-human, Jesus Christ. A literal reality underlies the metaphors when God became a human being with human characteristics.

The biblical writers seemed quite aware of the limitations of using human terminology to speak of God. For instance, in Deuteronomy 4:12, the writer says that God met Israel at Sinai. The people heard the voice and the words, but saw no form. In Exodus 33 when Moses sought a vision of God, he asked to be shown only God's glory—and even then the glory of God was seen only in passing. Yahweh said, "You cannot see my face, for no one may see me and live" (Exod. 33:20).

Isaiah, in spite of all his figurative language, flings out the compelling question, "To whom, then, will you compare God? What image will you compare him to?" (Isa. 40:18).

The same message carries though to the New Testament. "No one has ever seen God," declares John 1:18. When speaking to the woman at the well, Jesus said, "God is spirit" (John 4:24), which means that God has no physical form. Paul stated that God alone has immortality and "lives in unapproachable light, whom no one has seen or can see" (1 Tim. 6:16).

We have to use the kind of terms readily understood by people. Even when we make a simple statement such as "God sees my need," we are bringing God into our world.

We are acknowledging the God who cares. This makes us aware of the personableness of God, and we also sense divine compassion and love.

The best reason for using such terminology is that God, through the Bible, speaks to us in these terms. This is part of God's self-revelation to us. It's as if God says, "You can't possibly comprehend who I am, so I'll give you a few hints to guide your understanding."

We are—as the Bible clearly declares—made in the image of God and after the divine likeness. It makes sense that we use human terms to express this.

Our wisdom is a weak reflection of God's wisdom, and this is true for love or anything else in life. Even our bodies, our capacity to act, to express ourselves, to plan and make choices dimly reflect God's superior power, motives, and ability.

∞

Is it possible that the anthropomorphic language of the Old Testament was preparation for the human appearance of God, born as a baby in a stable? Isn't it possible that God spoke of hands, ears, feet, and heart as a way to set the stage for the moment in history when God would walk and live in bodily form?

The astonishing truth of the gospel is that ultimately God did take on human form, even to the extent of a totally human body that wept, experienced hunger, and felt anger.

Think of these verses:

- "The Word became flesh and made his dwelling among us" (John 1:14).

- Paul writes of Christ Jesus, "Who, being in very nature God . . . made himself nothing, taking the very nature of a servant, being made in human likeness. And being found in appearance as a man, he humbled himself and became obedient to death" (Phil. 2:6–8).
- "That . . . which we have seen with our eyes, which we have looked at and our hands have touched," wrote the apostle John (1 John 1:1).
- Jesus himself said to Philip, "Anyone who has seen me has seen the Father" (John 14:9).

When we speak of Jesus as God, we can speak in reverent tone of hands, feet, and eyes. We can contemplate divine love, compassion, righteousness, or even the holy wrath. We can do that because those verses make it clear that, in Jesus Christ, God assumed human form as the ultimate unveiling, the grand self-revelation.

CHAPTER 11

Present on the Scene

"Hey! Look, there's God!"

No one actually said that, but several times in the Old Testament we find examples of a God-sighting—a visible, physical appearance of the divine one. Sometimes God appears as a man and at other times like an angel. The writers make it clear that they believed such physical appearances were in fact God.

Theologians, who love to coin impressive words, call such appearances a *theophany* (*theos* = God; *phanos* = appear). The word doesn't come from the Bible.

Theophanies—God in visible form—come on the scene to communicate, to confront, or to reveal truth. Think about what an impact that would make for God to appear in some kind of visible, tangible form.

Theophanies are limited to the Old Testament and are most common in Genesis and Exodus, but they also occur in the writings of the prophets, especially in connection with the calling of a prophet.

We can classify the theophanies in several categories when God appears:

- directly to a person (Exod. 19:9–25),
- through a vision (Gen. 15:1–21),
- in a dream (Gen. 20:3–7; 28:12–17),
- as an angelic being, usually the angel of the LORD (Gen. 16:7–13; Josh. 5:13–15, and others), and
- as an angelic being in a dream (Gen. 31:11–13).

Such events were not common. Just the fact of a theophany was a way of waving banners and yelling, "God has a special message here!"

Consider the importance of the following God appearances:

- God appeared to Abraham in the form of three men and told him that his wife would have a son, Isaac, within a year (Gen. 18:10). This, then, began to unfold the great plan of Abraham's descendents being as numerous as the sands of the seashore.
- God called to Moses out of a burning bush (Exod. 3:2ff). This was the beginning of the deliverance of the Israelites from Egypt.
- Before Joshua led the Israelites into their first battle in the new land, a man with a sword appeared to him and Joshua recognized him as more than a man: "Then Joshua fell facedown to the ground in reverence" (Josh. 5:14).
- God wanted to deliver Israel from the cruel Midianites and he chose Gideon, who was from the smallest tribe and a nobody. God in human form commissioned Gideon to save the people (Judg. 6:11–24).

- Another deliverance story for Israel occurred when God appeared to a sterile woman and told her she would bear a son—Samson—who would deliver Israel from forty years of Philistine control. She was filled with doubts and ran to tell her husband. He came and also saw the "man of God" (Judg. 13:8).

Most of those human appearances were to Israelites. Two exceptions stand out. In a dream, God appeared to King Abimelech and showed him that Sarah was Abraham's wife and not his sister as the couple had told him (Gen. 20:1–6). The other instance happened when God spoke to a prophet of Moab named Balaam (Num. 22:20–35).

The Angel of the Lord

This Old Testament term appears several times, such as in Genesis 16:7; 22:11; 31:11. The most frequent, visible manifestation of God's presence is called the "angel of the LORD [Yahweh]."

With this physical appearance, the story is told in such a way that the person being addressed somehow knew that he or she was not talking to a mere mortal. They recognized they were in God's presence. Most of the time, those who saw this appearance had a powerful experience and declared that they had met God. The angel of the Lord does things that only God can do, such as forgive sins. Twice, the angel promised the birth of a male child to a barren woman.

The deity of this unique angel shows because:

- It was identified as God (Gen. 16:7).

- The angel was recognized as God (Gen. 16:9–13; Judg. 6:22–24).
- The terms used to describe this angel were words used only of God (Exod. 3:5, 14; Josh. 5:15).
- The angel said, "I am God" (Gen. 31:11–13; Exod. 3:2, 6, 14).
- The angel received and accepted worship—something God's angels don't do (Josh. 5:14; Judg. 2:4–5).
- The words spoken by the angel were words of divine authority (Judg. 2:1–5).

Many interpreters see the Old Testament theophanies as anticipating the New Testament event of Christ's incarnation and point to God being present among the redeemed.

Theophanies in Nonhuman Form

Exodus 3 describes Yahweh appearing to Moses in the flame of fire in a bush. This includes the sight of the bush as well as the voice of God speaking to Moses.

Another other-than-human appearance was the cloud in the daytime and the pillar of fire at night that led the Israelites during their wilderness journey and described God's presence with them.

God also appeared within a cloud to the people (Exod. 19, esp. verse 9). To a people ritually prepared at the appointed time, to the accompaniment of thunder, lightning, thick cloud (no article), and a continuing trumpet, Yahweh came down in fire upon the mountain to speak. The people were not allowed to go up; only Moses was allowed to do so.

Even in a theophany, people don't actually see God. This is impossible, according to the statements such as

Exodus 33:9, 1 Timothy 6:16, and 1 John 4:12. What humans see are forms or manifestations, as if God put on a human covering to communicate more effectively. The essence of God was present, but the physical sight was only an instrument.

One day such theophanies were no longer needed. Once Jesus Christ came to earth and lived a full human life, we never read of theophanies again.

CHAPTER 12

Understanding God's Mysterious Doings

We will always have many unanswered questions when it comes to understanding God. Even so, we keep asking. Part of being human is the inborn need to make sense out of life. This chapter focuses on three difficult words that have shown how the great minds through the centuries have tried to explain God's mysterious actions and involvement to help us make sense of life.

Theodicy

"Why is there so much evil in the world?"

"Why doesn't God do something about the wickedness around us?"

"If God is so good, why do bad things happen to good people?"

Such questions trouble many people today because some people have badly shaped ideas. For instance, deep within, they believe that if we serve God, our lives will be problem-free. Another mistaken attitude is that God's purpose is to make us happy. (In reality, our purpose is to honor and enjoy God.)

Jesus himself said that God "causes his sun to rise on the evil and the good, and sends rain on the righteous and the unrighteous" (Matt. 5:45). Life's troubles strike every one of us. To be free from difficulties doesn't mean that God is with us. As long as evil survives in this world, bad things will happen to good people, and good things will happen to the wicked as well.

Abuse, war, hurricanes, earthquakes, avalanches, random acts of violence, cancer, and heart disease are rampant in our country. Our relationship to God doesn't make us immune to these problems. The relationship offers us strength to cope.

The theological word to struggle with over this is *theodicy,* which is the realm of thinking about God's justice in spite of the existence of evil. Theodicy is sometimes called the vindication of God's goodness and justice despite the existence of evil in our world.

Haven't such questions troubled the world since Cain killed Abel? Jesus once asked, "Those eighteen who died when the tower in Siloam fell on them—do you think they were more guilty than all the others living in Jerusalem? I tell you, no" (Luke 13:4–5).

It's difficult to talk about evil because acts of evil in our time are major stumbling blocks to many people who can't understand.

First, there is no truly satisfying answer. We can start by referring to what we call natural law. This refers to the laws of nature and includes hurricanes, earthquakes, and tornadoes. When they strike a geographic area, they do so without regard to whether the people are followers of God.

Second, we can turn to moral law—the results of choices made by people. Most of us like to insist on the freedom of the will. This means people can make choices—good or evil. When they make evil choices, they bring destruction, chaos, and wickedness. Such decisions include war, crime, theft, rape, and incest.

Natural law doesn't seem as difficult to grasp. No one intentionally plans such problems. We admit that no one—other than God—can harness the forces of nature. We do, however, tend to ignore the fact that each of us may have helped to contribute to natural disasters by our abusive treatment of the environment. None of us is innocent. God told Adam and Eve to take care of the world. But we, their descendants, have polluted the atmosphere and raped the land. Smog and intense ultraviolet rays have resulted because we haven't treated God's creation well. We don't like hearing that, but perhaps we need to admit our complicity and guilt.

Moral evil is where most of us have the greatest problems. Why, many people ask, does God *allow* wicked people to make such choices of behavior? We can call it simply acting out our free will. Luther, Calvin, Zwingli, and other Reformation leaders insisted that because we're sinful by nature, our natural impulse is to do evil (see Ps. 14; Rom. 3).

Today, some of the leading minds in the world are speaking of the ripple effect of behavior or the chaos theory. They're saying that every time we take any action— even the smallest gesture or attitude—we affect others in their choices. Therefore, every action, no matter how small, has a ripple effect around the world.

The worst form of evil may not be the natural misfortune that happens to us, but that which we do to one another. We inflict problems, pain, and death on one another. The evil we do to one another has two significant facets: (1) It's always rebellion against God and the order of creation, and (2) it's against our fellow creatures. We call it sin, and we are guilty of much of the evil in the world.

Biblical teaching begins by declaring that God created a perfect world for the enjoyment of humanity. Because of sin and wrongdoing, humans began to pervert the world. They quickly learned selfishness and evil desires.

If serving God meant only getting good results, then it would be as if God bribed every follower—rewarding good people and punishing the wicked.

The example of Jesus Christ suffering pain, humiliation, and death—by God's command and intention—shows us that even the Holy One endured suffering.

The Bible teaches that eventually—at the end of the world—God will call all things into judgment, and we must answer for all our actions. In the meantime, Peter says that God "is patient with you, not wanting anyone to perish, but everyone to come to repentance" (2 Pet. 3:9).

The Bible makes no attempt to justify God, who is sovereign. God has willed the existence of both good and evil, and we believe that in the end, all works for God's glory.

Predestination

Predestination is another difficult issue to tackle.

Historically, Augustine (about A.D. 420) developed the idea of the need of divine grace while combating a teaching that overemphasized human power of self-determination. For three hundred years after the Protestant Reformation, this teaching was widely disputed. It produces less argumentation today. This theological term of predestination divided Christians, and it still troubles many. At its simplest meaning, predestination emphasizes the sovereignty of God over the human race.

Today, the advocates of predestination usually make two points in explanation. First, God, who is all-powerful, has predetermined the course of human history and the lives of individuals. This is much like Israel being the chosen people of the Old Testament—it was done by a sovereign decision to include one nation and to exclude all others.

Second—and here's where the discussion comes in—God's predestination of human events doesn't eliminate human choice. (Some people stand on a doctrine often called "irresistible grace" that denies freedom of choice; this isn't a popular position and is held by only the most devoted followers of reformer John Calvin.)

Obviously, the question arises: "If God chose some people, why didn't God choose all?"

Without getting into theological arguments, the Bible doesn't support the notion that God plays favorites or blesses certain people while cursing others. God did choose Israel, but they were to be a divine light to the nations. True, they didn't provide much light, but that was their failure. Providence (see p. 83–84) emphasizes a divine ordering and regulation of the world and history toward a

positive goal. Predestination emphasizes a predetermina-
tion of human destiny in conformity with an eternal plan.

Beyond any question—and even the most radical prede-
terminist would agree—the gospel of salvation through
Jesus Christ is freely offered to everyone. Christians struggle over the acceptance of that salvation, and I don't think
there's any way to resolve it.

The conflict comes down to this: Did God, before the
literal creation of the world, already choose certain people
for salvation? The most vocal supporters of predestination
say, "Yes. All were sinners and on their way to destruction.
A merciful God snatched some out of the fires of hell."

Those who argue against the doctrine say, "Hey, wait.
It's a gospel freely offered. If it's freely offered, then God
doesn't make the decision. Only people can choose."

The arguments can go on indefinitely—as they already
have and will. We finally have to say, "If those theologians
and scholars haven't resolved it in two thousand years, I
can live with not knowing."

No matter which position we gravitate toward, all of us
finally come down to saying, "We choose to follow Jesus
Christ."

Christians *do* agree that creation is moving within the
purpose of God—even though we may not understand
everything this implies. The Bible says, "In him we were
also chosen, having been predestined according to the plan
of him who works out everything in conformity with . . .
his will" (Eph. 1:11). A few verses earlier, Paul wrote, "For
he chose us in him before the creation of the world to be
holy and blameless in his sight" (Eph. 1:4).

I'll try to sum up today's major views on predestination.

1. *Augustinian (or Calvinist) view.* This view places the emphasis on God's predetermined wisdom. It says that God decreed human salvation from before the beginning of creation. Salvation, however, isn't contingent upon human action or work but solely on grace. This grace God showered on the human race without human merit. Those who are divinely elected will believe and follow God. God is the only one who knows who is chosen.

Positively, this position emphasizes:

- the sovereignty of God,
- God's love is freely given and never earned or deserved, and
- salvation comes from God alone.

Negatively, this position assumes that once, long ago God planned everything that would ever happen to everyone who would ever live. If that's so, then world history and the history of every person becomes simply the predetermined, unalterable unwinding of a long book written before the world began. God wrote the book, retired from the scene, and became only a passive observer of a pre-fixed world process. It also implies the end of human freedom.

The real question is this: Is the source of this teaching really God's self-revelation and will, or is it an illegitimate speculation based on how a sovereign God would and should act?

It also seems to me that we have to look at the other side. If some people are predetermined to eternal life, guess what happens to the rest of the human race? Right! They're predetermined to eternal damnation—often called double predestination. This double predestination turns the good news of Jesus Christ into bad news, at least for some people.

2. *Universalism.* This is the other extreme. Salvation includes everyone. God is so loving that none will perish. God chooses all and rejects none. No matter who they are or how strongly they reject God, ultimately—and that's the key word, *ultimately*—they are destined for a life of joy and peace with God, along with everyone else in the world. (Some people would say that they might suffer for a time, but it's only temporary.) This position was condemned early in the history of the church as heresy. It has never been an acceptable position among Christians.

3. *Pelagianism.* This view is so called because of the teaching of Pelagius, against whom Augustine first formulated the doctrine of predestination. Jacobus Arminius (1560–1609) proposed it again and soon gained a following. Today, it may be the most accepted view among Protestants.

We can express this position in many ways. "It's up to you" is one way. Another is to say that God chooses those who choose God. If we turn to God, God turns to us. God's love, help, and salvation are *available* to every soul in the world, but they are *effective* only to those who ask. Another way is to say that Jesus Christ achieved *potential* salvation, but it becomes *real* salvation only for those who believe.

Positively, Pelagianism/Arminianism emphasizes the following:

• People make decisions about their relationship to God.

- This stands with Old Testament passages such as Deuteronomy 6:25 ("And if we are careful to obey all this law before the LORD our God, as he has commanded us, that will be our righteousness").
- God's favor is based on obedience (see Isa. 1:19).
- Those who call, God hears and saves (Acts 2:21).

This involves God's foreknowledge (knowing in advance). By using that foreknowledge, God knows who will believe in Jesus Christ and faithfully follow, but God doesn't determine their salvation. This view emphasizes the responsibility of each person to hear and obey God's offer. Salvation, then, takes place only after a human response. God's grace is the source of redemption, but it can be resisted through free choice.

One person said, "If we take the first step forward, God rushes to us and carries us the rest of the way."

Negatively, Pelagianism/Arminianism emphasizes the following:

- This position questions the sovereignty of God.
- The Bible speaks of God's demanding a response but never that he will or can do anything until humans take the first step.
- In biblical history, it is God, not people, who initiates the saving events from the Exodus to the resurrection of Jesus Christ.
- This position questions the love of God. In effect, it says, "I'll love you if you love me first."

Providence

The word *providence* never appears in the Bible, but the effect is there. If we focus on the idea of God *providing,* we stay close to the meaning. It is the continuous activity within creation by which God preserves and governs the world. Providence implies the following:

- The universe can't continue if left to itself.
- All life depends on the will of God.
- This dependence applies not only to existence but to the quality of life.
- A supreme intelligence operates everywhere in nature.
- The moral and spiritual nature of humanity demands a corresponding and controlling providence.
- The fulfillment of promises and prophecies in the Bible are founded on this concept.

Providence (often mistakenly called predestination) means that God's absolute rule or sovereignty includes all creation. This, then, denies that chance or fate governs the universe. The Bible teaches that God controls the universe, the physical world, and even the affairs of nations ("He rules forever by his power, his eyes watch the nations," Ps. 66:7).

Providence means the provision and protection of those who belong to God. He acts in accordance with the laws and principles he has established in the world.

I like to say it this way: The laws of nature are human descriptions of how we perceive God at work in the world.

God preserves all things through divine providence. Without God's continual care and activity, the world wouldn't exist. This continued activity of God directs all things to the ends he has chosen.

CHAPTER 13

The Contract Maker

The word *covenant* isn't one that most of us use today. We find it occasionally in financial transactions. Otherwise it's a word limited to the theologically literate.

If we try to define the word, we usually end up with a definition something like this: "An agreement between two people or two groups that involves promises on the part of each to the other."

The idea of the covenant between God and people—usually Israel—signals an important event in the Bible. It denotes an agreement that binds them mutually to undertakings on each other's behalf. Theologically, it denotes a gracious undertaking entered into by God for benefit and blessings, specifically for the people of faith who receive the promises and commit themselves to the obligations this involves.

Although there are many covenants mentioned in the Bible, there are two major ones, called old and new. This becomes clear to anyone who picks up an English Bible. The first section is called the Old *Testament*—another word for covenant. Beginning with Matthew's Gospel, the rest of the books are part of the New *Testament*.

A general characteristic of ancient covenant is that the parties considered them unalterable—that is, permanently binding. They obligated themselves—in the sense of vowing—to carry out their commitments under penalty of divine retribution if they didn't.

Often the promise was supported by some sort of legal consideration. When one party of the agreement was socially or financially superior to the other, the situation differed. For instance, a king would announce what he considered best to impose on his people. The people, unable to do much else, expressed acceptance and readiness to conform to the "agreement." Without saying so, however, by implication, the king would promise to rule for the best interests of his people and to protect them against enemies.

There are differences, however, when God initiates the covenant. The one-sided effect becomes even stronger. Those who accepted the covenant stood in an inferior position. The covenant constituted a divine announcement of God's holy will to extend the benefits of unmerited grace to those who were willing to receive it. By entering into a commitment to God, they bound themselves by ties of absolute obligation.

The characteristic statement of the relationship occurs in the formula, "I will be their God and they shall be my people" (cf. Jer. 11:4; 24:7; 30:22; Ezek. 11:20; 14:11; Zech. 8:8).

When God made covenants, this wasn't unusual. In the ancient Middle East society, covenants were an important part of life. They didn't always use the term, but their activities implied mutual obligation—which is the idea behind the word. Such mutual obligations took place within the family, within clans and tribes, and especially between nations and their gods or between nations that held treaties with each other.

The Old Testament gives accounts of covenants between persons such as Laban and Jacob (Gen. 30:25–43) or David and Jonathan (1 Sam. 18:3).

The important biblical use of the covenant occurs when it involves God. To understand the Old Testament idea of covenant, it helps to focus on the word *loyalty,* although the covenant carried an even richer meaning. Exodus 34:6 reads, "He [God] passed in front of Moses, proclaiming, 'The LORD, the LORD, the compassionate and gracious God, slow to anger, abounding in love and faithfulness.'" The words "abounding in love and faithfulness" express God's behavior and attitude toward those in covenant relationship. Consequently, loyalty often says it well; when we apply the term to God, covenant includes the divine love that is unchanging and totally reliable.

In covenants, the greater power demands loyalty but obligates itself to protect the lesser, such as when Israel agreed to a covenant with the otherwise-defeated Gibeonites (Josh. 9). Most of the references to covenants in the Bible refer to this type of treaty, especially the covenant that God, the greater power, made with Israel at Sinai.

The first significant covenant in the Old Testament is the one between God and Abraham and was followed by a ceremony (Gen. 15:9–17).

At Sinai, God demanded, as was the custom in such treaties, that the people accept all terms given to them, even before they knew what they were.

This same idea appears in what we call the new covenant. God calls Christians to follow obediently and without reservation. When believers through the ages make such a commitment, we have no idea what such loyalty or obedience will mean. As the weaker in submission to the higher power, we consent to the terms. We do this because God's love was shown to us through the death of Jesus Christ. All through both Old and New Testaments, God unequivocally promises to bless the lives of those who obey.

Covenant Overviews

Here is an overview of the major covenants of God in the Bible.

1. *Noah.* In this covenant, God promised Noah never again to destroy the world by flood (Gen. 9). This is unusual in that there are no conditions to this agreement.

2. *Abraham.* This father of the Hebrews was to remain faithful to God and to serve as a channel through which God's blessings could flow to the rest of the world (Gen. 12:1–3). This covenant is much like those granted to loyal servants by a king as a reward for faithfulness and loyalty.

3. *Moses or the Sinai Covenant.* The people of Israel would have understood this as a type of king-to-vassal agreement. In the Hittite treaties during that period, the main elements included:

- The covenant began with the name of the treaty maker, that is, the great king.

- The document had a historical introduction and included prior benefits provided by the great power.
- It listed the people's obligations to the king.
- A list of divine witnesses followed.
- A litany of blessings and cursings came after that.
- The entire covenant was read aloud to the people.
- The people agreed to the conditions.
- After that, the people ate a ceremonial meal.
- They concluded by laying the treaty at the feet of their idol.

The mosaic covenant is similar, although not done in exactly the same order.

- Yahweh, the great king, is the covenant maker.
- God reminds Israel of their deliverance from Egypt (Exod. 19:4–6; 20:2).
- The people hear the stipulations or conditions (Exod. 20:3–23:33).
- The witnesses are "heaven and earth" (Deut. 4:26; 30:19).
- Blessings and curses are listed in Leviticus 26 and Deuteronomy 27:11–28:68.
- Moses read the covenant to the people (Exod. 24:7).
- After hearing the terms of the covenant, the people said, "We will do everything the LORD has said; we will obey" (Exod. 24:7).
- The Passover meal became an annual observance (Deut. 16:1–8).
- They placed the treaty (the Ten Commandments) inside the ark of the covenant (Exod. 25:16; 40:21).
- In addition, the people of Israel are called the children of God, which speaks of a family relationship.

4. *David.* In this covenant, God promised that if David and his descendants remained faithful they would be established forever on the throne of Israel (2 Sam. 7:12).

Although the Bible doesn't specifically lay down the conditions, the covenant obviously depended on their obedience to the Sinai covenant (1 Kings 2:4; 8:25). All through the Old Testament, the prophets emphasized obedience to the covenant of Sinai as necessary for the continued existence of Israel in the land. Because the people repeatedly violated the terms of the covenant, the land was taken from them and they went into exile.

5. *New Covenant Promised.* After the destruction of Jerusalem and beginning of the Exile, God promised a new covenant (Jer. 31:27–37). This new covenant differed from that given to Moses and the Israelites. This coming one would be internal ("This is the covenant I will make with the house of Israel after that time, declares the LORD. 'I will put my law in their minds and write it on their hearts'" Jer. 31:33).

6. *New Covenant.* The term *new* reminds readers of the older covenant of the law and the many ways God dealt with people throughout history.

The covenant was enacted when Jesus the Messiah, a descendant of the line of David, met with his disciples on the night before his crucifixion. They ate bread and then he gave them the cup of wine to drink and said, "This cup is the new covenant in my blood, which is poured out for you" (Luke 22:20).

All followers of Jesus became members of the new covenant. The New Testament Book of Hebrews makes the greatest use of covenant language (see, for example, Heb. 7:22; 8:8–13; 9:15; 12:24).

In Summary

After the disobedience of Adam and Eve (see Gen. 3:1–20), sin entered the world, and God prepared the way for human salvation. God's method has been to enter into a covenant with humanity.

Throughout the Old Testament, God made covenants with individuals. Each agreement expressed God's grace toward humanity and centered on delivering them from the results of sin. Beginning with the promise to all humankind that a universal flood wouldn't occur again, the divine pledges narrowed down to a specific people— the Israelites. God made a covenant with Israel. Because of their repeated disobedience, God offered a new covenant. By the death of Jesus, God entered into a new agreement— open no longer primarily to Jews first, but to all who would obey Jesus Christ.

The new covenant achieved what the Mosaic covenant couldn't do. The old covenant (the law) pointed to a way of life, but it didn't give the power to live it. God's laws are now written upon the hearts of the covenant people, and they are empowered by the Holy Spirit.

CHAPTER 14

Spiritual Beings and God

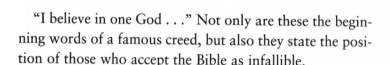

"I believe in one God . . ." Not only are these the beginning words of a famous creed, but also they state the position of those who accept the Bible as infallible.

Although the Bible clearly states that God is one, and that there is no other god, the Bible readily acknowledges other spiritual beings. Some of those beings are unholy competitors who fight against truth and godliness. It's important to notice that the archenemy of God, called by various names such as the Devil or Satan (see chapter 25), is not an equal.

That is, the Bible doesn't teach dualism. Here's a picture of what I mean by dualism. Some people see themselves as being pulled by God, who grabs one hand and the Devil grabs the other. The two powers are equally strong, so it's a toss-up over who will win the soul. Such a concept never appears anywhere in the Bible.

The idea of two mutually hostile forces or beings in the world does have ancient roots. The most clear-cut idea of this came from Zoroaster of the ancient Iranian religion.

Zoroaster and his followers envisioned the world as a battleground for opposing forces of light and darkness. When Jews returned from their years of exile in Babylon, many brought with them a belief in Satan. Although never made equal to Yahweh, the concept of Satan does become the great adversary to turn people from true worship.

Christianity and Judaism have never considered dualism acceptable. The Bible teaches that the Devil ultimately will be excluded from the universe. If that being were equal with Yahweh, such a thing couldn't happen. Dualism holds that the Devil is eternal and independent of the divine will. Because the Bible teaches that God is totally sovereign, we cannot accept dualism as possible.

The bigger objection to me is that dualism robs us of the ethical character of sin. Dualism would say that sin comes about apart from our inner natures and desires. That would mean we sin because we're caught between two opposing forces. Such a belief diminishes human responsibility for sin.

Yes, Yahweh is one God and there is no other. That's a basic belief all through the Bible. Even so, the Bible also speaks of other spiritual beings—those who are not human. Here are brief pictures of those other-than-human beings in the Bible.

Angels

The word in both Hebrew and Greek means messenger, and it can refer to human or supernatural beings. Although they often have the appearance of males, they are genderless and "neither marry nor be given in marriage" (Matt. 22:30).

What do we really know about angels?

Not much, really. Most of what we hear and read today comes from sources outside the Bible. For instance, the Bible doesn't speak about our having an individual, guardian angel.

Most of the language in the Bible about angels comes largely in poetic or symbolic language as in Psalms, Daniel, and Revelation. The use of symbolic language makes it difficult to interpret such passages.

Because they are heavenly beings, it's difficult to describe angels in human terms. If we take the passages about angels literally, we learn that they spend most of their time praising God (Ps. 103:21; 148:1–2). They remain at God's side, ready to fulfill every command or mission given them (1 Kings 22:19).

Gabriel and Michael are the only angels named in the Bible, and they are involved with delivering divine messages. Some scholars believe that Michael's task is to care for Israel (see Dan. 10:13, 21; Jude 9; Rev. 12:7). By contrast, Gabriel is to bring special messages, such as those given to Mary and Joseph before the birth of Jesus.

The Bible strongly asserts that we are not to worship angels. In fact, angels point others to worship the true God.

When we think of angels primarily for their function as divine messengers, as the word suggests, it makes it easier to grasp their place in the Bible. They made significant announcements of good news to:

- Abraham (Gen. 18:9–10),
- Joseph in a dream to tell him to marry Mary (Matt. 1:20–25),

- Mary that she would bear a son (Luke 1:30), and
- shepherds to announce the birth of Jesus (Luke 2:8–15).

They also warned of coming dangers (Gen. 18:16–19:29; Matt. 2:13). The Bible also speaks of God's angels sent to destroy or take human life, as in Genesis 19:13 and 2 Samuel 24:16.

Here's a summary of facts we glean from the Bible about angels.

- They never speak to a wicked person or one who opposes God.
- They appear to the great saints of God such as Abraham, Moses, David, Daniel, Jesus, Peter, and Paul.
- They appear in human, male forms (Gen. 18:2; Dan. 10:18; Zech. 2:1).
- Sometimes they appear in dreams, such as to Jacob (Gen. 28:12; 31:11) and to Joseph (Matt. 1:20).
- When they visit people, they inspire awe (Judg. 13:6; Matt. 28:3–4; Luke 24:4).
- They care for people in times of need (Ps. 91:11–12; Heb. 1:14).
- They guide and teach people (Gen. 24:7, 40; Exod. 14:19).
- They protect and deliver God's people (Exod. 14:19–20; Acts 5:19; 12:6–11).
- They relieve hunger and thirst and provide for human need. For instance, an angel saved Hagar's life in the desert (Gen. 16:7).

Angels, Fallen (or Demons)

These are heavenly beings or divine messengers, created by God, who rebelled. Here are the statements about them in the New Testament:

- They are "kept in darkness, bound with everlasting chains for judgment on the great Day" (Jude 6).
- They continue to serve Satan but have limited power.
- They are cursed by God and will go "into the eternal fire prepared for the devil and his angels" (Matt. 25:41).

Cherub, Cherubim

We have no idea what the word *cherubim* means, but they are described as winged, angelic beings, often associated with the worship of God. They are mentioned ninety-one times in the Old Testament, only once in the New Testament (Heb. 9:5).

The term probably represents a variety of beings. The only feature regularly found in the references is that they are winged creatures. Beyond that, the details vary. For instance, the ark of the covenant had two cherubim facing each other and they each had one face. In Ezekiel's temple, they had two faces; in Ezekiel's vision, they had four. At no place in the Bible are they ever presented as chubby-faced children that we commonly see in art.

Genesis 3:24 is the first mention of cherubim in the Bible when God has them drive Adam and Eve from the Garden of Eden. They were posted at the garden with "a flaming sword flashing back and forth to guard the way to the tree of life."

Cherubim are always connected with God. Psalm 18:10 pictures God as mounting and flying on cherubim.

When the Israelites built the tabernacle, they made representations of cherubim. Two were made of gold and placed at either end of the mercy seat, above the ark of the covenant. Artistic designs of cherubim decorated the ten curtains and the veil of the Tabernacle.

Devil

This is the English translation of *diabolos,* which means "accuser" or "slanderer." It is used in the Greek version of the Old Testament (the Septuagint) to translate the Hebrew word *Satan.*

Several descriptive phrases in the New Testament apply to the Devil by referring to the being's wicked personality or deeds. Here are some of them:

- *Wicked or evil one.* This phrase shows his fundamental nature is to oppose everything about God in every way (Matt. 13:19, 38; 1 Pet. 5:8; 1 John 2:13).
- *Enemy.* This term refers to the one who tirelessly tries to uproot good, as in Matthew 13:25, 28, 39.
- *Murderer.* This was a term Jesus used of Satan in John 8:44.
- *Deceiver.* Since the Garden of Eden, this has been one of the most common tactics of the Devil (see Rev. 20:10; 2 Tim. 3:13).
- *Beelzeub, prince of demons.* Although religious leaders accused Jesus of doing deeds that were actually conducted by the Devil, the term is ancient. In the Old Testament, the term referred to the god of the Philistines (Matt. 9:34; 12:24; see 2 Kings 1:2–3).

- *Ruler* or *prince of this world.* This term was used three times by Jesus (John 12:31; 14:30; 16:11).
- *Tempter.* (Matt. 4:3).
- *Prince of demons.* (Luke 11:15).

Demons

The word originally referred to any one of numerous, vaguely defined spirit beings. In the New Testament, they are understood as evil spirits who oppose God and God's people. These are heavenly beings or divine messengers, created by God, who rebelled. They continue to serve Satan but with limited power, and ultimate judgment awaits them.

In ancient times, people believed that demons caused sickness, both physical and mental, and calamities of nature such as earthquakes and storms. They were the forces responsible for much of human sin and always worked to oppose God.

Satan

This word means "adversary," and many interpreters consider Satan the personal name of the evil one. Satan and the demon cohorts represent the powers of evil in the universe. It is against this power that Jesus came to fight and to establish the kingdom of God.

In the New Testament, Satan appears frequently, especially in the Gospels. In Revelation it becomes clear that no matter how powerful Satan seems, the final overthrow is certain (Rev. 20:1–10).

Much of the modern teaching about Satan comes from *Paradise Lost* by John Milton (1667). For instance,

Isaiah 14:12–14 and Ezekiel 18:12–15 are addressed to the kings of Babylon and Tyre. But largely because of the influence of Milton, many believe that they refer symbolically to Satan being cast out of heaven.

In the New Testament, only one passage could be taken to refer to Satan as an angel who was cast out of heaven because of rebelling against God. Jesus said, "I saw Satan fall like lightning from heaven" (Luke 10:18).

Seraph, Seraphim

Among the heavenly creatures comes this term that means "fiery or burning ones." They were angelic or heavenly beings associated with the prophet Isaiah's vision in the temple when he was called to his prophetic ministry (Isa. 6:1–7). This is the only reference in the Bible.

Isaiah described seraphim as having six wings. They used two to fly, two to cover their feet, and two to cover their faces. The seraphim flew about the throne on which God was seated, singing praises. In this instance, they served as God's agents of purification. One placed a hot coal against Isaiah's lips and said, "Your guilt is taken away and your sin atoned for" (Isa. 6:7).

CHAPTER 15

Problems with Sin

——————— ∞ ———————

None of us likes it, but the Bible states that we're sinners before we ever do anything wrong. The moment we're born, God labels us sinners.

The Bible primarily shows sin as being against God, even when the wrong we do is to others or to ourselves, such as the prayer of David after committing adultery with Bathsheba, impregnating her, and killing her husband to cover it up: "Against you, you only, have I sinned and done what is evil in your sight" (Ps. 51:4).

The idea behind sin begins with God as the lawgiver. Hence, sin is anything contrary to the expressed will of God.

According to the Bible, life wasn't always that way. God created the human race without sin, morally upright and ready to do good. Then the world turned upside down when Adam and Eve disobeyed God's command and ate of the forbidden tree of the knowledge of good and evil. The tree wasn't the issue, but they disobeyed the command of God.

This was the start of sin. From then on it infected the entire human race. That is, Adam sinned not just as one man, but as the representative or father of the human race. Paul argued that Adam represented all of us. Therefore, Adam's guilt gets passed on to every person born in the world. The proof of this statement is the reality and inevitability of death. If we weren't sinners, we wouldn't die: "Therefore, just as sin entered the world through one man, and death through sin, and in this way death came to all men, because all sinned" (Rom. 5:12).

We're all declared guilty sinners in Adam the same way God declares all believers righteous in Jesus Christ. (That's another big argument Paul makes—Adam's failure plunged us into sin and Jesus' perfect sacrifice pulls us out.) Associated with that is what we call the corrupted or sinful nature that passed from Adam all the way through the human race. No one is free from sin (see Rom. 3:23; 6:23; Ps. 14).

An older term we don't hear much today is *total depravity.* Particularly during the period of the Reformers and Puritans, they used the term to impress on their hearers that the contagion of sin spread throughout the entire human race and left no part of us untouched by sin. They wanted to make certain we learned the truth of the power of sin within us and that we had no recourse or way to save ourselves.

The Bible defines sin in several ways. It is lawlessness or not obeying God's will (1 John 3:4)—either by omitting the right thing or doing what God forbids. This failure can come through our thoughts (1 John 3:15), our words (Matt. 5:22), or the things we do (Rom. 1:32).

Because God demands righteousness, sin also refers to the failure of our relationship with him. Breaking God's law at *any* point becomes sin at *every* point, argues James 2:10.

The Bible pictures us as dead—killed spiritually by sin (Eph. 2:1). Then it goes on to say that we are alive only through the sacrificial death of Jesus.

Sin began with disobedience. Adam started it and our disobedience, although different, amounts to the same thing. The Greek word for sin, *hamartia,* means to miss the mark, to be less than perfect.

Biblical writers had a keen awareness of sin and looked upon it as no less than a condition of dreadful separation from the Holy One. They knew that apart from God, all of us are lost sinners, unable to save ourselves or find genuine happiness.

This awareness is so keen that it's difficult to find chapters that don't make some reference to what sin is or what it does. We can easily make a case that the Bible has two major themes—sin and salvation. We constantly find ourselves engaged in sin and then we suffer its painful effects, but God steps in and offers deliverance.

The Bible also shows the development and human understanding of sin. From the earliest pages of the Bible after the introduction of sin, people show an awareness of it. Adam and Eve knew they were naked and clothed themselves. Cain was troubled over killing his brother. And the stories go on. As people learned more about Yahweh and the ongoing plan for humanity, their recognition of the seriousness of sin also developed. The prophets preached the tragic reality of the nation's sin. The destruction of

Jerusalem by Babylon, perhaps as much as anything else, made them aware of their utter sinfulness and their total forsakeness of God's laws.

The Old Testament awareness of sin presents a rich vocabulary to describe sin. Here are some of the words used.

- The most common root is a word that means "to miss" or "to fail." Most of the time when the word is used, it refers to spiritual and moral failures toward others or God (see Gen. 20:9; Lam. 5:7). Sometimes the word included the guilt and punishment accompanying sin, as in Genesis 43:9.

- The most common theological word means "to revolt, rebel, or transgress." It's not merely a mistake but a willful, deliberate act of defiance against God. This idea lies at the heart of the Genesis account of the beginnings of sin. The essential problem lies in the desire of humans "to be like God." All sin is an act of idolatry—the attempt to replace the Creator with someone or something else, usually themselves or something they have created.

- There is the sin of ignorance—doing something wrong but not being aware of it.

- Another reference means "to wander" or "to stray," which is similar to ignorance.

- Another word means to refuse to obey Yahweh's commandments and is found in such passages as Exodus 4:23.

- To be godless or profane is still another term and it indicates ruthless violation of anything that's holy.

Sin brings an estrangement from God. Hence, anyone was then "polluted."

- To act treacherously indicated sacrilege or apostasy from God.
- Still another word means to be or to act wrongly through conscious and intentional badness.
- The opposite of the word "to be righteous" is another term, and it means "to be guilty or wicked." Despite sounding like a judicial word, it also indicates the corrupt inner nature of the guilty (as in Ps. 1:4: "The wicked . . . are like chaff"). In Isaiah 57:20 sinners are described as being like the tossing sea. This shows the vivid imagery associated with the word.
- The name of Belial is another term, and it refers to the worthlessness and unwholesomeness of the godless (as in 1 Kings 21:10 KJV).
- The word usually translated "be bad" or "be wicked" carries a strong ethical tone.
- "To treat violently or wrongly" is still another descriptive word used for sin.
- Several words refer to the results of sinful action. One such word means "toil, trouble, mischief," and it indicates the sorrow caused by the wicked (see Job 4:8).
- Other words, found especially in the Psalms, are associated with deceit, lying, and malicious slander (see Ps. 64:2).
- Generally, the Hebrews didn't distinguish between sin and the resulting guilt. Most of the major words for sin mentioned above also carry the idea of guilt.

This list doesn't exhaust the vocabulary of sin in the Old Testament. Other words show sin's actions such as pride, folly, backsliding, deceit, and uncleanness.

Old Testament Conclusion

Other than Genesis 3, where Satan tempts Adam and Eve, there is virtually nothing else in the Bible about the origin or source of sin. Instead, the writers trace the acts of sinfulness within the human race.

According to Old Testament writers, especially Jeremiah, sin comes from the corrupt human heart— the center of our being—and that center is at odds with the Holy Creator.

For Old Testament writers, the heart isn't the center of the intellect, but more the center of the will—and the human will has become corrupt. God showed humanity the right way and made a covenant with Israel, but they refused to obey and continually rebelled. Because sin is rooted inside the human heart, all of human life is tainted and no activity is exempt from it. We can talk about religious sins, social sins such as pride, hatred, and envy, but it really means that sin resides in the intentions and desires (Exod. 20:17).

God warns against giving in to sin and urges us to do good and to leave evil. Each of us is also held responsible for our personal wrongdoing. From the basic idea of idolatry derive most of the other ideas connected with sin.

New Testament Conclusion

In the New Testament, the emphasis is on an even closer relationship between God and humanity. The message is that through Jesus the realm of God has come, our sins have been forgiven, and a new relationship has been established that eventually will bring the hopes of all the biblical writers to fulfillment. This will be accomplished through the work of God in Christ to break the enslaving power of sin and liberate people. We participate in this struggle to defeat sin in our lives.

CHAPTER 16

Why Did Jesus Die?

Ask anyone who's been to church more than twelve times why Jesus died, and the answer comes easily: "Jesus died for our sins."

Good answer. Not a full answer, but it's a beginning. It still doesn't answer the *why* question. Why did Jesus have to die for our sins?

Then we answer, "Because we're sinners and have displeased God."

Good answer again but still not enough.

In fact, the theologians have discussed and argued this question for centuries. They refer to Jesus' death and all the results of that death as the *atonement.*

But that's not the end of the discussion. Although theologians agree on the basic facts, they aren't in agreement on the purpose and result of the atonement.

Atonement, which means "to make amends," is another of those terms not found in the Bible. We use it to refer to the perfect and completed work of Jesus Christ by which he offered himself to bring us to God.

We know that the atonement happened, and we understand the results—salvation for humanity, life eternal, the daily presence of God—and the list goes on. *But why did it happen that way?*

Here's the real question to grapple with: How can God be just, faithful, and righteous to the divine nature and still justify disobedient creatures? (We're the disobedient creatures.) Let's try it another way. Sin deserves punishment and condemnation. So how can a holy God accept sinners without violating divine holiness or sentimentalizing love into an indifference to wrong?

I start once again by stating that the atonement is something we don't fully understand. Some of the great thinkers in the church have formulated theories to explain this event. The New Testament paints vivid pictures that operate in our imagination to make real to us the saving truth of redemption in Jesus Christ's self-offering on our behalf.

Here are the major theories or ideas great thinkers have come up with to explain the necessity of Jesus' dying on the cross. I think there's something in each of them worth pondering.

Recapitulation or Reversal Theory

An early church leader, Irenaeus (about 130–200), viewed this as a question of justice. By Jesus' human birth and perfect life, he *reversed* the course of action started by Adam and carried on by all his offspring. That is, he undid the actions of the original couple.

Thus, Jesus communicates life everlasting to those united to him by faith. The life we receive transforms us ethically. Jesus Christ as the second Adam reenacted human experience. The death of the innocent one in place of the guilty, Irenaeus said, wrested the human race from the grasp of the Devil. That action opened the possibility (not the assurance) of a holy, obedient life for mortal sinners.

Irenaeus's theory dominated the church's thinking for nearly a thousand years.

Ransom-to-Satan Theory

OK, it's never been the number one theory in popularity, but it has hung in there for a long time. About two hundred years after the crucifixion, Origen (about 185–254) formulated this idea of compensation to the Evil One. He said that God paid a ransom to cancel the just claims that Satan held on humanity. Origen also said that when human beings disobeyed God, Satan, the adversary, demanded the souls of sinners. Because all humanity sins, eventually Satan got us all. But God outsmarted Satan by paying for the sins of all humanity through one person— Jesus the Christ.

For the next thousand years, scholars found vague references to Origen's position in writings, but it wasn't ever commonly accepted.

Satisfaction or Commercial Theory

This idea started with Anselm (1033–1109). It emphasized the absolute necessity of Jesus' death by tying it in with God's nature. Human beings owe their Creator complete obedience. When we don't totally obey every rule of God, that's sin. Sin, by definition, is disobedience and an aggressive act against God. We rob the sovereign Creator of divine honor.

Anselm then went on to say that God couldn't just show mercy and forgive. God's self-vindication came by remaining faithful to the divine nature. This meant that some other action had to happen to satisfy God's honor—satisfaction that could only come from the disobedient race.

God could have handled it in one of two ways—by punishment (God could punish every one individually for sin) or by satisfaction (some form or method that would "satisfy" God's honor).

Which did God choose? That's easy. God is merciful, which is part of the divine nature, so God chose satisfaction. This satisfaction came in only one way, which was through the death of Jesus Christ. Anselm said it was the only way because God's honor needs an infinite satisfaction.

When Jesus came to earth, he fully obeyed every command of the Law of Moses, which God had laid down as duty for all. That, in itself, was not enough. In addition, the one who committed no sin had to suffer and die in doing his duty. Because Jesus was sinless and under no obligation to suffer, and especially to die, that sacrifice brought infinite glory to God—which was its purpose.

Along with this, Jesus' death merited a reward. But, since he was sinless and the Son of God, Jesus had no need for reward. He then passed it on to humanity in the form of forgiveness of sins and of future blessedness for those who obey God's commands.

Critics have charged that this is a rather mechanical system. It ignores the love of God, which is crucial to the understanding of the New Testament. Positively, this theory emphasizes the magnitude of sin and recognizes that either satisfaction or punishment is mandatory because of sin. Anselm wanted a rational, logical basis by looking at the nature of God.

Moral Influence Theory

Abelard (1079–1142), in opposition to Anselm, proposed that there is no principle of the divine nature that necessarily calls for satisfaction. Jesus' death shouldn't be seen as payment for sin but as a manifestation of God's love, suffering in and with sinful creatures, and Jesus taking on himself their griefs and failures.

Jesus' suffering wasn't to *satisfy* divine justice but to *reveal* divine love to soften human hearts and, thus, lead them to change. Abelard believed this love assures sinners there is no obstacle on God's part to prevent their being pardoned for sin. God not only does this without receiving satisfaction, but he also does it eagerly and from unfathomable love. This theory requires only that sinners come to God with penitent hearts.

For Abelard, the great love of God frees us from the fear of wrath so we can serve God in love. Everything in the atonement demonstrates God's love through the cross. When humans perceive this love, almost automatically, it draws out their love for God.

Abelard has had many argue against him. They say the atoning work of Christ is not primarily to reveal God's love but to satisfy divine justice. Someone said that it reduces the saving event to a "tragic martyrdom."

The Dramatic Theory

During the Protestant Reformation, Martin Luther developed what is called the dramatic theory, but it took John Calvin's analytical mind to say it systematically. Largely, they agreed with Anselm that the atonement is rooted in the nature of God, but divine *honor* wasn't the issue. They said divine *justice* had to be satisfied. If humanity is to be redeemed from the curse of sin, a sacrifice must be offered. God offered the sacrifice of Jesus. Christ took upon himself the punishment for all sinners. Thus, the sacrifice satisfied God's justice and appeased the intended wrath or punishment.

In working out this theory, Calvin pointed to Jesus in three offices—prophet, priest, and king. Jesus saves us by performing on our behalf the functions proper to each of those offices. As priest, he appeases God by his offering himself. After Jesus returned to heaven, he continues to intercede perpetually for God's people.

∞

Other theories come and go, but these are the ones that have remained. Obviously, sincere Christians disagree on the explanation of the atonement.

I wouldn't try to give a definitive answer to the question. However, I can suggest several things to think about when we ask, "Why did Jesus die?"

1. Because I accept the Bible as the ultimate truth, I believe that Jesus Christ died for sinners—and I am one of those sinners.

2. As I understand the Bible, personal relationships constitute the essence and provide meaning. This means that the Bible emphasizes the personal relationship between the

Creator and humanity. The heart of the reconciliation lies in restoring that which was lost—relationship lost because of human sinfulness. (That's another way of saying the atonement is about forgiveness.)

3. We have to keep in tension that God is holy. Although holy, God is love and loving. That love wills to take away human suffering that we, the creatures, have produced. Thus, far from negating the basic truth of divine love, the death of Jesus discloses it. Sin isn't the end, but God's love that submits to all that sin can do, and yet does not deny itself.

4. All creatures are sinners. Through the misuse of our freedom we have alienated ourselves from God and incur both guilt and wrath.

The Bible portrays us many times as being in the dreadful state of humanity without Jesus Christ.

- We're slaves who need to be redeemed.
- We're enemies who need reconciliation.
- We're corpses that need to be resurrected.
- We're captives who need to be freed from our oppressors.
- We're criminals who need to be justified.

5. When holiness faces human sin, the situation demands God's wrath. The New Testament shows wrath as well as mercy coming from God.

Even though I write that statement, we need to see wrath properly. It's not sinful vindictiveness or a mean God getting even. Instead, it may help if we think of God's love as an attitude concerned about personal relationship. When divine love doesn't elicit love in return, there is—as even parental affection shows—a reaction of pain, anger, and estrangement.

If we eliminate the possibility of divine wrath, someone has said, "We flatten God's love into a subpersonal indifference." If we see grace as part of the nature of love, then grace has meaning.

6. In resolving the human dilemma in rescuing us from our predicament, God, through the death of Jesus, carries out an action that has eternal effects. Hence, all the startling biblical pictures—drawn from the marketplace, slave trade, military campaign, temple sacrifice, or law court—are essential.

No matter what New Testament picture we focus on, the writers saw the death of Jesus as an act that secured forgiveness of sin. Paul's major picture of the atonement is the law court, which he refers to several times in Romans. He uses the language of the judicial system to show that God doesn't act like human judges. Instead God uses grace to nullify the divine law by accepting the death of Jesus Christ.

7. This leads us to the fact of substitution, and there is no understanding of the atonement without it. Jesus Christ the perfect One identifies with us in love and we—in faith—identify with him.

8. We can't deny or ignore the penal aspect of the atonement. Jesus became the object of retributive justice and bore our punishment. This goes back to Isaiah 53:6 and says that Jesus took the penalty for sin upon himself. In this aspect, the punisher and the punished are one.

The New Testament pictures the atonement objectively. That is, it's a work accomplished outside of human involvement. It has been done for us at a specific time in history. Jesus' death, in ways we may not fully understand, reconciles us to God. The atonement didn't change the divine nature; it did change our relationship with God.

Being like God

We're not God, but we're the closest picture of the divine one on earth. We know this because of the words the Creator spoke on the sixth day of the earth's beginning: "Then God said, 'Let us make people in our image, to be like ourselves. They will be masters over all life—the fish in the sea, the birds in the sky, and all the livestock, wild animals, and small animals.' So God created people in his own image; God patterned them after himself; male and female he created them" (Gen. 1:26–27 NLT). (The translators say "in our image, to be like ourselves." Virtually all translators agree the two terms mean the same thing.)

In short, we were created in God's image. Theologians love to talk about this by using the Latin phrase, *Imago Dei*. Maybe it just sounds better.

What does all that mean? We're not angels; we're not animals; and we're not just things. We're the finale of God's drama of creation. Sounds wonderful, doesn't it?

So what does it mean to be the image of God?

The Bible makes it clear that before sin entered the world, the first humans were still perfect. In Genesis 3 is the story of Adam and Eve deliberately disobeying God. We call that the "Fall." We can say they fell into sin or they fell out of grace. The point is, they disobeyed and learned that they would have to die.

So where does that leave us? After the Fall, did humanity lose that sacred image? Was it only marred? Is it still totally intact?

As I see it, the real problem comes when we look at the effect of sin. If human sin alienated us from God—as we find spelled out in so many places (Ps. 14; Rom. 3)—our reasoning says it must have changed our likeness as the image of God. God is the all-perfect, sinless one, and by humans being declared sinful, weren't we changed? If we didn't lose all of the divine image—and I don't think anyone suggests that—are *marred* or *blurred* the best words to express our status today?

That's where the differences of understanding arise. No thinkers want to say we totally lost divine likeness. We're no longer what we were created to be, but parts of our nature are still recognizable as being God's image. But which parts?

This has been a favorite battleground through the centuries. For one reason, there is such a brevity of biblical information. One thing seems obvious: The Bible proclaims the resemblance of some important character between humanity and the divine nature. Most important to remember is that God exalted humanity above all other creatures.

In the first chapters of Genesis, the human race stands apart from everything else created. We have two unique things said about us. First, we have "dominion" over all living things and, second, God told us to "subdue" the earth. One way to think of this is that God created us to be the earth's caretakers.

Many overlook the personal aspect of God here. The human race doesn't get thrown into the fields with the words, "Get to work." We're first created in God's likeness and then we're told to subdue the earth. I like to think of it this way: God creates and humans govern. (OK, we haven't always done a good job, but that's the ideal.)

If that's the case—that we're God's caretakers—then we need to be equipped for the task. We have to be able to think and to act. We also need the ability to reflect.

In the second account of creation (Gen. 2:4–25) we see the human relationship with God, who placed the couple in the garden "to work it and take care of it" (Gen. 2:15). Another way to say it is that what God created becomes human responsibility to maintain.

Very early we also see Adam's sense of self-awareness. He realized he was alone and had no mate like the other creatures. Self-awareness is the ability to feel and to reflect. It's a quality we still have—although it's imperfect.

Here are the major viewpoints about the image of God in man.

1. *Imago Dei refers to human reason, will, and personality.* God is a person, self-aware, the supreme intelligence, and totally free. Humans are also intelligent, rational, self-conscious, and free to make choices.

2. *Imago Dei means human spirituality.* Because God is Spirit, this likeness appears in our spiritual nature— our ability to respond and relate to God.

3. *Imago Dei is present only when individuals are in relationship with God.* The image is present like a reflection in a mirror, rather than like a photo—a permanent print image. This says that once people belong to God, they grow more like Jesus Christ.

4. *The Image of God is something we do.* Immediately after God created humanity in the divine image, the couple received dominion or authority over the earth. This view says that the active tending and caring for God's creation constitutes the image of God in human beings.

So which one is right? I don't know. It probably involves all of them. We know that human beings—and only human beings—have personal, conscious fellowship with God. We're to take God's place (that is, represent God) in ruling over and developing creation. Yet these activities are possible only because of certain qualities of personality that only we, of all God's creation, possess.

Perhaps to be in God's image means we have the ability and the privilege of knowing, serving, and loving God. We are most fully human when we have fulfilled our spiritual potential.

I like to think of it this way: We are created with personhood. We were created for relationships and also created to need them. In the Garden of Eden, God placed the first couple in four basic and enduring relationships: (1) to God, (2) to others, (3) to the world, and (4) to themselves.

Too many people have focused on what's lost through sin—and that usually speculatively—instead of what it still constitutes. The Bible makes it clear that we have suffered the loss of righteousness and purity, but it also points to grace as the force to renew such qualities, although not to fully restore them.

CHAPTER 18

And God Said . . .

God spoke and people heard and then responded. That's basic in understanding the Bible. Nowhere in the entire sixty-six books of the Bible is there ever a question about whether God communicated directly with individuals. The question was whether those who said, "Thus says the Lord" really had heard from God. The Bible carries strong admonitions against false prophets who proclaim their own message as a word from God. One of the Scriptures' strongest statements reads, "If a prophet, or one who foretells by dreams, appears among you [and tries to lead you astray] . . . you must not listen to the words of that prophet or dreamer . . . that prophet or dreamer must be put to death" (Deut. 13:1, 3, 5).

In the final days of Jerusalem when false prophets insisted that God would deliver, only Jeremiah's voice proclaimed that the city would be destroyed. "This is what the LORD Almighty says: 'Do not listen to what the prophets are prophesying to you; they fill you with false hopes.

They speak visions from their own minds, not from the mouth of the LORD'" (Jer. 23:16).

All through the Bible, the faithful prophets denounced those who falsely claimed to speak for God. In the midst of such stern warnings, we infer that God continued to speak, otherwise there would be no need for such denunciations.

"Yes, but *how* does God speak?" becomes the pressing question, followed by, "How did they know it was God?"

The Bible never answers these questions, although we have ample illustrations of God communicating with individuals, mostly faithful followers. The prophets often began their message by saying, "Thus says the Lord." It was their way of stating clearly that they had heard from God and were communicating a divine message.

Typical of the writing prophets is the simple, "The word of the LORD that came to . . ." (Joel 1:1). Obadiah called his message a vision. Sometimes prophets called it an oracle. Regardless of the terminology, those who heard God speak made it clear they knew the source.

The Bible does not explain how God spoke to people like Noah, Abraham, Moses, or David, but the Bible does declare that they received divine messages. As the biblical accounts move forward, the human voice of a prophet becomes a significant medium. In a number of biblical accounts, especially after Israel settled in Canaan, God spoke through prophets to provide national and individual guidance.

For example, King Ben-Hadad and his armies besieged Samaria, the capital of the Northern Kingdom. Because the people had no way to get food supplies, famine broke out. To die or surrender seemed the only alternatives. Then

Elisha said to the people of the city, "Hear the word of the
LORD. This is what the LORD says: About this time tomor-
row" (2 Kings 7:1). He then stated that food would be
abundant and the prices cheap. To an official who
opposed him, Elisha predicted, "You will see it with your
own eyes . . . but you will not eat any of it" (2 Kings 7:2).

Abruptly the enemy fled, "for the Lord had caused the
Arameans to hear the sound of chariots and horses and a
great army" (2 Kings 7:6). The people crushed the official
when they stampeded to get the foodstuff the Arameans
had left.

We can't eliminate dreams and visions as significant
methods of communication in the Bible, although most
Christians today raise an eyebrow over them or even scoff
at such an idea. Yet in ancient civilizations, people
accepted dreams as words to them from God. Often those
dreams came symbolically, such as Pharaoh's dream of
seven fat cows being eaten by seven starving cows.

In the generation after the resurrection of Jesus, we find
an enormous amount of supernatural activity and divine
communication going on with the disciples. Healings were
common, and so was God's spoken word.

Two early members of the Jerusalem church deceived
Peter. The apostle obviously had received some kind of
message from God, because there was no way he could
have known. When Peter denounced them, they were
struck dead (see Acts 5:1–10).

In 1 Corinthians 12 and 14, Paul wrote at length about
the spiritual gifts. Sandwiched between the two chapters
is the famous love chapter of 1 Corinthians 13. By that
insertion, Paul said that as important as it is to have God

speak, without being motivated by love for God and for one another, such revelations are nothing. In chapter 14, he explained how they were to manifest those gifts. For example, no one speaking a message in tongues (an unknown language) could do so without an interpreter being present. If prophets wanted to speak, two or three should do so and "the others should weigh carefully what is said" (1 Cor. 14:29).

More than once Paul spoke of his own revelations and understandings (see 2 Cor. 12; Gal. 2:2).

Acts 13 lists a number of prophets and teachers who were praying and fasting at Antioch, the scene of the first missionary outreach of the church. "The Holy Spirit said, 'Set apart for me Barnabas and Saul for the work to which I have called them'" (Acts 13:2). We assume this came through one of the prophets, but it isn't made clear. My assumption is that such events as God speaking through a human instrument were so common in the early church that Luke didn't bother with details.

Yes, God spoke in times past. Anyone who believes the Bible has no problem accepting that statement. From there, it naturally leads us to ask, "How does God speak today? How do we know when it's God and not just our own thoughts or imagination?"

Christians differ when it comes to the matter of God speaking today. Most believe that God communicates with individuals, although maybe not as clearly or as directly as in the past. They would then go on to say that God answers prayer or guides in a variety of ways. A few, especially charismatic Christians, believe that God has begun to restore spiritual gifts. Among them are prophets or those who pray and give words of guidance from God. They are a minority.

Although not denying that God provides ongoing guidance in some form, most Christians speak a cautionary word: God speaks, but never in contradiction of what's in the written Word. That's a wise reminder.

Here are the ways many Christians experience God speaking today.

1. The most commonly accepted method happens when Christians read the Bible. God sometimes makes a verse or a story come to life. "It was as if I had read that verse for the first time," I've heard many longtime Bible readers say.

2. Being open to hear the message of preachers and teachers is another way God speaks. My first experience of this happened about a year after my conversion. I sat in a Sunday morning worship service in San Antonio, Texas. For a couple of days, I had been thinking about my life before I had turned to Jesus Christ and some of the things I had done and the friends I associated with. There was a kind of nostalgic feeling; I even considered writing to one of them.

Just then Pastor Bell had been preaching from Philippians 3:13, "But one thing I do: Forgetting what is behind and straining toward what is ahead." Mentally, I had nodded off when his voice cut through my introspection. "Looking back means going back," he said.

When he uttered those words, I heard them as clearly as if God had shouted to me from the highest heavens.

My experience wasn't unique. When preaching and teaching are at their best, that's one way God says a loving word, points a convicting finger, or guides a discouraged soul. Instead of the written Word, he speaks through the proclaimed word of God.

3. God also directs through circumstances. Actually, that's one reason the casting of lots prevailed throughout Bible days. The people prayed and believed that when they asked God a yes-or-no question, they would receive divine guidance.

I don't think we use that method today, but when the once-closed door opens, we often see this as God speaking to us through circumstances.

4. Others testify of having heard God speak to them through words of wisdom and guidance from others, such as in counseling situations or in fellowship with other believers.

5. The difficult one is what I call a mystical experience. Over the years, I've talked to people who told me they had asked God for guidance and afterward, they "just knew" the answer.

For example, a never-before-published friend named Suzanne Stewart wrote a book. Several of us helped her with the writing and prayed with her for guidance. One day she calmly stated God had given her an answer. She knew the publisher and was going to send it to them. I urged her to contact several.

"No, this is the one. They're going to accept it." Suzanne knew, and it wasn't a matter open for discussion. She was correct, because within weeks, she had an acceptance from that publisher.

Even today, Suzanne couldn't explain that knowing— only that it was an inner certainty that precluded doubt.

I've also had such an experience, and I think it's common among many Christians.

6. Sometimes God speaks in unusual ways, such as through a hymn or a poem. My father-in-law had gone to church for years, but the message had never sunk in. One evening he sat beside his wife and the service closed with an old gospel hymn, "There's a New Name Written Down in Glory (and It's Mine)." As the congregation sang the words and he read them in the hymnbook, he began to weep. God had spoken. He knew he needed to surrender to Jesus Christ. God guided him through a hymn in a way that no preaching or teaching had done.

If we ask people, "How does God speak today?" they would have a difficult time answering. It may be that, as we see in the Bible, there are specific periods when the divine directions come readily, as when the Jews wandered in the wilderness, or during the early days of the message of salvation through Jesus Christ.

Finally, however, most of us would say definitely that God speaks. We don't know and we can't always figure out the way. Many of us still pray, "Speak Lord, for your servant listens." The methods may not be as dramatic or as powerful, but somehow the Lord does communicate with us.

CHAPTER 19

God's People Today

─────── ∞ ───────

What is the Church? When I capitalize the word *church*, I go back to the Greek word, which means "called out." We can define the Church as a community of people called out of the world to be the people of God. The Church isn't an institution but a supernatural entity that's in process of growth. It's the sphere of the action of the risen Christ. All believers are linked together by the Holy Spirit.

Characteristics of the Church

If a local congregation truly represents God at work in human lives, these are the characteristics that mark or display the work of God among them.

1. *The Church preaches the Bible.* This is the most important characteristic. Christians have always stood for the proclaiming of God's Word. This doesn't mean that the preaching must be perfect, but it's a striving for purity of doctrine and a faithful presentation of the truth from the Bible.

2. *The Church rightly administers the ordinances (or sacraments).* Divorced from the Bible, the ordinances have no content of their own; they only derive meaning from the Word of God. Baptism and the Lord's Supper, the two ordinances/sacraments accepted by most Christians, are sometimes called the visible preaching of the Word.

3. *The Church is God's agent of forgiveness, renewal, and judgment in the world.* We're not only to be a fellowship to comfort and encourage one another, but we are people with a divine mission—to speak to the world around us by our actions as well as our words.

4. *The Church disciplines its members.* Although many congregations ignore or downplay this aspect, leaders of the past have insisted that purity of doctrine and guarding the holiness of the sacraments are essential. The Church cannot be the true Church without disciplining its own members. The Bible strongly speaks of this aspect (see Matt. 18:18; 1 Cor. 5:1–5, 13; 14:33, 40; Rev. 2:14–15, 20).

The Early Church

In the early New Testament period, Christians began in the synagogues and from there they worshiped in homes. Their times together seem to have had little structure and remained flexible to meet changing needs. As the Church became better established, believers focused on ways to accomplish its mission.

From reading the New Testament, we can't discover one pattern or form of government in the early Church. During the early period, the apostles directed the work at the headquarters in Jerusalem. The people chose seven men to assist with members' needs, and we usually refer to them as the Church's first deacons. This was the beginning of church government. Later, the offices of evangelists, pastors, teachers, elders, and bishops emerged.

The first Christians formed a closely knit community in Jerusalem. After the Church began to carry the gospel outside Jerusalem, Philip went to Samaria and Peter visited the major cities of Israel, preaching to both Jews and Gentiles. Others went to Phoenicia, Cyprus, and Antioch of Syria, and the gospel spread throughout the then-known world.

Initially, Jesus' followers apparently saw little need to develop a system of church government. They dealt with internal problems as they arose—usually in an informal way. By the time Paul wrote letters to various congregations, Christians had begun to organize. The New Testament doesn't give much information about the structure. Apparently, one or more elders (or presbyters) presided over the affairs of each congregation, just as elders did in synagogues.

Some congregations appointed deacons to distribute food to the needy or care for other material needs. There are a few references to the leadership of bishops in the early Church. Paul seemed to have used the terms *elder* and *bishop* interchangeably and charged them with the oversight of a congregation.

As the early Christians worshiped together, they established patterns of worship that were quite different from the synagogue services. We have no clear picture of early Christian worship before A.D. 150, when Justin Martyr described typical worship services in his writings. When

Christians were persecuted, they met in secret places such as the catacombs (underground tombs) in Rome.

Early Christians ate the symbolic meal of the Lord's Supper to commemorate Jesus and his disciples observing the traditional Jewish Passover feast. The themes of the two events were similar. In the Passover, Jews rejoiced that God had delivered them from their enemies, and they looked expectantly to their future as God's children. In the Lord's Supper, Christians celebrated their deliverance by Jesus from sin and expressed their hope for the day when Christ would return.

Baptism was a common event of Christian worship. It appears that the early Christians interpreted the meaning of baptism as a symbol of death to sin (Rom. 6:4); cleansing from sin (Acts 22:16); and new life in Christ (Rom. 6:3). Occasionally the entire family of a new convert would be baptized. This may have signified their desire to consecrate all they had to Christ.

The Church was a single worldwide fellowship of believers, and Paul described the Church as "one body in Christ" (Rom. 12:5), because it includes all who are united to Christ.

The early Christians also identified themselves as the new Israel, God's chosen people (see Gal. 6:16), because God had established a new covenant with Jesus' followers (2 Cor. 3:6; Heb. 7:22; 9:15).

How Did We Become So Many Groups and Denominations?

Jesus commanded his disciples to go throughout the entire world and to preach the good news, beginning in Jerusalem (Acts 1:8).

As the gospel spread, so did the problems. Even the emphasis of the message changed; it was no longer the Jewish religion with the added dimension of faith in Jesus as the Messiah. A council of the leaders in Jerusalem made the official decision (see Acts 15) that believers would no longer have to go through Jewish rituals. Even after the decision, dissension frequently arose. Paul's letters tell of the difficulties in the churches he founded.

If we realize there was a lack of full unity at the beginning, we can see how denominations began. Here are two examples.

1. For the first three centuries, Christians argued over the nature of Jesus Christ. Was he just a man with an inspired message? Was he God who only appeared to be human? Until the first ecumenical council at Nicea in A.D. 325, the churches of Jesus Christ had no official position.

2. When Emperor Constantine moved his capital from Rome to Constantinople (now Istanbul) in 330, he planted the first seeds for the most important split of the Church. Until then, believers in the East and West had united as the one Church. In the East, four patriarchs were of equal status with the pope of Rome.

Those in the Eastern Church spoke Greek; Latin was the language of the West. After the Goths invaded Rome, the Church of the West appealed to the Franks for help instead of to Constantinople. In gratitude for his aid, the pope of

Rome crowned Charles the Great the emperor in 800, and the Western Church became identified with the Holy Roman Empire.

Conflict deepened between the Eastern and Western Churches. The final split came when the West added the word *filioque* to the Nicene Creed.

Briefly, the Eastern Church held that the Holy Spirit proceeded directly from the Father; the Western Church contended that the Holy Spirit proceeded from the Father *and* the Son—*filioque*. In 1054, the pope excommunicated the eastern patriarch. He, in turn, excommunicated the western pope. This split meant the formation of two distinct Christian organizations, both claiming to be the true and faithful followers of Jesus Christ.

Today Christendom is divided into three major sections: Roman Catholic, Eastern Orthodox (often called Greek Orthodox, although there are Orthodox Churches in other nations), and Protestant—which represents all groups that don't fit under the first two. Because members of the Western Church founded the congregations in the new world, the American continents have remained with the West.

Yet even the Western Church wasn't ever truly united. All through the centuries, individuals arose who differed from official teachings, cited abuses, and preached against wrong emphases.

Before Martin Luther's break with the Church in 1517, other voices had protested—many of them dying for what they believed. Individuals such as John Wycliffe (1320–1384), John Huss (1369–1415), and Savonarola (1452–1498) stand out. The infamous Spanish Inquisition and the Catholic Counter-Reformation came into being to silence those dissenting voices.

Denominational Structures

As the Church spread throughout the world, structures and patterns became more formalized. Two thousand years later, we can identify the three basic forms of Church structure—all of which can trace their beginnings back to the early days of the primitive Church.

These three structures are episcopal, representative, and congregational.

1. *Episcopal.* The word *episcopal* is from a Greek word that means "bishop" or "overseer."

This form of church government regards bishops as a distinct office higher than pastors or elders. Each bishop has jurisdiction over a number of congregations and their officers. This form is often called a rule by bishops, because they are the authority in local congregations and in the denomination. The Church of England follows an episcopal system with the head of state also the head of the church.

Aside from the churches with the word *episcopal* in their name, the Roman Catholic Church exemplifies this system. Roman Catholics view the church as the continuing visible presence of Jesus Christ in the world. Christ maintains his life on earth through the Church. The clergy form a hierarchy that governs the church, with the pope as the highest authority.

The pope is the bishop of Rome, and Roman Catholics believe that the papal office has been passed from pope to pope. To Roman Catholics, this authority originated in

Christ's declaration of Peter as the first pope. They base this on Jesus' words: "And I tell you that you are Peter [which means rock], and on this rock I will build my church, and the gates of Hades will not overcome it" (Matt. 16:18).

2. *Representative.* A board of elders or presbyters governs churches in this category. (*Presbyteros* is the Greek word for "elder.")

In this system, elders, who are elected by the congregation, make most of the decisions regarding the operation of the church. Generally, they're part of a series of graded courts: presbyteries rule over local congregations in a geographic area; synods rule over presbyteries in a geographic area; and the general assembly decides on issues affecting the entire church. This is the system used by denominations with the word *Presbyterian* or *Reformed* in their name.

3. *Congregational.* The congregational system, in its purest form, recognizes no human authority having jurisdiction over more than a single local congregation. This is fairly close to a democratic government in which all members have an equal voice.

Congregational churches include Baptists and those with the word *congregational* in their names. It also includes the Society of Friends (Quakers), who reject any type of church ruler or official and almost every form of physical organization. Even though many congregational-type denominations have ties to other churches, they still hold to the sovereignty of the local fellowship.

In the new millennium, many people wonder about the assortment of denominations. As long as the Church of

Jesus Christ remains on earth and as long as individuals have the right to speak their consciences, we'll probably never have a united church on earth. We can and will have a united fellowship in Jesus Christ that transcends those differences.

CHAPTER 20

God's Purposes

One day I discovered that Mark, who had been my friend for years, was dyslexic. That discovery made other things fit into place, such as he never wanted to read aloud and always laughed about being a poor speller. Now I knew. Although his situation had always been there, it was a revelation to me.

That moment of understanding works similarly to what we call progressive or historical revelation. Until people have the facts and can put them together, the reality remains hidden. Elements of the divine plan have moved steadily toward fulfillment from the first day of creation.

God didn't give Adam all the information and insight on the sixth day of creation. Over a period of centuries, the great planner has handed it out in small portions, always leading humanity toward a greater understanding of the character of God and of the divine plan.

The word *revelation* translates a Greek and a Hebrew word, both of which refer to an "uncovering" or "disclosing." Revelation in the Bible is shown as an unveiling of what was already true but unknown.

I find it helpful to think of the resulting knowledge as a gift rather than as a product of human analysis or study. Such revelations start when God speaks to chosen individuals, such as the New Testament apostle and especially the prophets in the Old Testament, who then transmitted their newfound insight to others. "Surely the Sovereign LORD does nothing without revealing his plan to his servants the prophets" (Amos 3:7).

Progressive revelation allows us to know only the tiniest amount of what lies ahead. However, once reality has come, we can look backward and realize the seeds of understanding had been planted in the past.

From the early third century B.C. and onward, the revelatory experience became an important element in what we call apocalyptic writings—writings about the end times, such as those of Daniel and Revelation. The prophet's powerful experiences enabled them to learn and reveal things to come. They never saw the whole picture. What they saw was true but incomplete. We don't have the complete picture and we won't until after the events have taken place.

The best way for me to explain is to think of Israel's dream of the Messiah. The people thought of him as one who would deliver them from their oppressors. By the first century A.D., they expected a military man who would defeat the Romans. In fact, the last question the apostles asked Jesus before his ascension shows how clearly this idea had permeated the nation. "So when they met together, they [the apostles] asked him, 'Lord, are you at this time going to restore the kingdom to Israel?'" (Acts 1:6).

Those men—Jesus' closest allies—still hadn't grasped that he was not going to bring about a military victory but an internal one. From all we can grasp of the New Testament, Jesus will come back with mighty armies and overthrow evil, but we have only a vague picture of how this will take place. (See chapter 34 about the end times.)

The easiest way to show this concept is to point to a few specifics.

1. God's most significant revelation occurred in Jesus Christ. Through the centuries, God had spoken, hinted, implied, and prepared the way for the deliverer. Many didn't recognize Jesus as the promised Messiah because they hadn't read the signposts along the way.

Passages such as Isaiah 53 take on significant meaning for us once we understand that Isaiah was pointing toward Jesus.

2. Next to the gradual revealing of God's plan to send a Savior into the world in human form, the most significant unfolding reaches its disclosure in the Book of Ephesians. That revelation also stirred up endless problems within the church because not everyone understood.

The revelation began when God called Israel to be a light to the nations. They never faithfully carried out that part of their mission to share the love of Yahweh with their neighbors. In fact, too often, the religion of their neighbors replaced or integrated with the true faith of Israel.

Look at the New Testament progression. After Paul met the resurrected Christ on the road to Damascus, he was blinded for three days. To Paul, the persecutor of Christians, God told a reluctant Ananais, "Go! This man is my chosen instrument to carry my name *before the Gentiles and their kings* and before the people of Israel" (Acts 9:16, author's emphasis).

That was a revolutionary statement to Jews who considered themselves—and only themselves—as God's people. Jews despised Gentiles and considered them worthless in the sight of God. They referred to them as "dogs," a sign of loathing. They often understood God's plan was to annihilate such dogs (see Isa. 60:12; 45:14).

Paul didn't immediately get the full impact of that message to go to the Gentiles. Like the other early Christian leaders, he preached to the Jews. Only after they rejected him did he offer the gospel to Gentiles. In time, Paul became the apostle (or ambassador) to the nations.

This mission to the Gentiles was the next step in progressive revelation. That, in itself, was amazing to Jewish believers—that God loved Gentiles as well as them. That revelation caused much misunderstanding and persecution.

Paul's revelation went further. When he wrote to the Ephesians about a great "mystery," he revealed the fulfillment of God's intentions—that all people—Jews and non-Jews alike—would be united to form the church, or as Paul says, "one new man."

Here are Paul's words: "In reading this, then, you will be able to understand my insight into the mystery of Christ, which was not made known to men in other generations as it has now been revealed by the Spirit to God's holy apostles and prophets. This mystery is that through the gospel the Gentiles are heirs together with Israel, members together of one body, and sharers together in the promise in Christ Jesus" (Eph. 3:4–6).

This is the great long-hidden secret of salvation—that Jesus Christ died for *all* humanity—something we take for granted now. Even a casual reading of the Acts of the Apostles shows that it took many years for Jewish believers to accept non-Jews without their converting to Judaism.

In the Book of Galatians, Paul argued that when Gentiles come to Jesus Christ, they don't have to go through Jewish rituals such as circumcision. Their faith in the Savior is all that God requires.

3. From the earliest pages of the Bible, humans offered animal sacrifices to God. The Jews learned that without the blood of an animal being sacrificed for sin, there was no forgiveness. That shedding of an animal's blood occurred on the annual Day of Atonement.

Christians don't need to go through that ritual, because we accept the perfect and eternal sacrifice of Jesus, who died as the Lamb of God (see John 1:29). Once the historical event of Jesus' death took place, the old system was no longer needed.

4. The role of women in the Old Testament, reflecting the time and culture, defined women in a lower state than today. However, in ancient Israel, women could inherit property. This put the Jews a step ahead of their neighbors.

Paul speaks of women not braiding their hair with gold, wearing their hair long, keeping silence, and they weren't allowed to teach men. This same apostle, however, also wrote Galatians 3:28: "There is neither Jew nor Greek, slave nor free, male nor female, for you are all one in Christ Jesus."

Many people see this as the verse that spells out the equality of gender. For the past thirty years or so, we in the church have been trying to merge that into our biblical understanding. Although everyone doesn't agree, most people have seen this as a logical progression. God gives a clue, a verse, a thought, and eventually the historical revelation clicks into place and becomes the norm.

5. Eternal life is hardly mentioned in the Old Testament. The reward of the faithful in ancient Judaism consisted of three things: (1) they would live long; (2) they would have many children; and (3) they would prosper—their land would be fruitful.

A few hints occurred earlier, but it was not until the Book of Daniel—written after the Jews had been conquered by the Babylonians—that a clear statement occurred about what happens after death: "Multitudes who sleep in the dust of the earth will awake: some to everlasting life, others to shame and everlasting contempt" (Dan. 12:2).

The New Testament speaks quite frequently of life after death. Paul's final chapter of 1 Thessalonians addresses the return of Jesus Christ, and 1 Corinthians 15 describes our bodies in the life-after-death experience.

6. In spite of differences of interpretation of the Book of Revelation, virtually everyone agrees that at least the last two chapters refer to the end of this world as we know it. Such teachings, called "eschatology" or "end times" (see chapter 34), are part of progressive revelation; God has a

plan that moves slowly into place. The end of that still isn't clear in its specifics, but the everlasting union with all believers and Jesus Christ is.

The focus of progressive or historical revelation is that God continues to speak and to give understanding of divine plans. Only as we move forward can we look back and say, "So that's what it means!"

CHAPTER 21

Behold! God at Work

God had a plan from before the human race existed. Consequently, the Bible isn't a book of history, science, or social studies. It's a book that focuses on the working out of God's eternal purposes.

God, for no reason that is ever explained in the Bible, chose Israel as a special people to work through. Although they didn't always understand (or obey even what they did understand), Yahweh's plan had already sped into action.

One way to understand God's relationship with humanity is to focus on the mighty acts of God through human history.

The Old Testament

1. *From Creation to Abraham.* According to Genesis, the first book of the Bible, God made the world and everything in it within the space of six days and declared it "to be very good." On the seventh day, God ceased from creating.

God created a man (Hebrew, *Adam*) and then a mate for him and placed both of them in a garden called Eden. Then they received a mandate—sometimes called our cultural mandate—to have dominion over the animals and the land. They had one negative command: They were not to eat fruit from the tree of the knowledge of good and evil. They already knew good. If they disobeyed, they would also know evil and be participants in doing it. We might think Adam and Eve wouldn't have any trouble obeying this commandment. But the Bible says Satan, in the form of a serpent, lied and seduced Eve into eating the forbidden fruit, and she shared it with Adam.

Both sinned against God, and from then on, everyone in the world has been called a sinner. At the beginning of the misery, God promised to send a Redeemer, also called a Savior or a Messiah, to destroy Satan (see Gen. 3:15, the first promise in the Bible of the Messiah or Christ).

The Bible begins the story of how God accomplished this plan of salvation. Because the Bible focuses on that one aspect of world history, it tells us almost nothing of people and events outside the scope of this salvation history.

Several important things happened between the time of Adam and that of Abraham, the "father of all who believe" (Rom. 4:11). For example, the first murder occurred. Adam and Eve had many sons and daughters (Gen. 5:4), although the Bible names only three (Cain, Abel, and Seth) because only they are important to the history of redemption. A jealous Cain killed his brother Abel and was punished by being driven away from the community of people who served God.

From then on, evil increased. By the time of Noah (Gen. 6), wickedness had become so rampant that God decided to send a great flood to punish sinful humanity and start again with one man and his family. This was the most important event of the ancient period. Noah built an ark (a large wooden ship) into which he and his family brought every species of animals and birds.

The flood came and it rained for forty days and nights, and every living creature on the earth died, except those inside the ark. After the flood, God put a rainbow in the sky as a promise never again to destroy all human beings by water.

Noah's three sons and their wives then began to repopulate the world. Chapter 11 of Genesis says that wicked people tried to get to heaven by building a tower in Babel. God condemned their ways by breaking them up into different language groups and scattering them to different areas of the world. Thus, the large language groups of the world began.

These events show us that evil continued to increase from the time of the flood to Abraham. During this period, ancient people worshiped many gods, and immorality was rampant. God, intent upon saving humanity, decided to begin anew by starting with one man and through that man, Abraham, all families of the earth would be blessed.

2. *From Abraham to Moses.* God chose Abraham as the first in the human line that eventually would bring salvation to the rest of humanity.

Abraham lived in the city of Ur, capital of the ancient kingdom of Sumer. Some time around 2000 B.C. God called Abraham to leave his father's home and go into a new land. The Bible traces Abraham's steps from Ur all the way to Canaan, and he was promised a son. Through that son, Isaac, Abraham's descendents would grow into a great nation and bless the peoples of the world. God also promised to make Abraham's descendants a blessing to all nations.

Abraham believed God, but as time went on and nothing happened, he apparently had doubts, so he took matters into his own hands. Because he and Sarah had no son, he fathered a child by his wife's servant, Hagar. The Muslim world of today looks upon that son, Ishmael, as their spiritual heir back to Abraham.

Although the ancient world accepted this means of securing an heir, it violated God's plan for a son through Sarah. Thirteen years after Ishmael's birth, when Abraham was 100, at age 90 Sarah gave birth to Isaac.

Abraham came to trust God more completely as the years went by. The man's big test came when God told him to offer Isaac as a burnt sacrifice to prove his love for God. An obedient Abraham prepared to kill his son, but God stopped him. Abraham then offered a ram for a sacrifice instead of Isaac.

Isaac had twin sons. The younger, Jacob, tricked his brother Esau, the firstborn, who should have been the rightful heir and the one in whom the divine promises would find fulfillment. From here on, the Book of Genesis turns its focus on Jacob and his descendents. God chose Jacob to inherit the promises first given to Abraham and confirmed to Isaac. This happened about 1850 B.C.

Jacob lived a troubled life—mostly because of his own misdeeds. God changed Jacob's name to Israel, and thus begins the history of the chosen people.

Jacob/Israel had twelve sons. The eleventh son, and his favorite, was named Joseph. His jealous brothers sold him as a slave to traders. Those traders took Joseph to Egypt and resold him. After several years in Egypt, which included a prison term despite being innocent, Joseph interpreted Pharaoh's dreams when no one else could. He told the king that Egypt would have seven years of abundant crops followed by seven years of drought, and they should store the excess produce during the years of plenty. Pharaoh accepted the answer and gave Joseph power, second only to his, and put him in charge of collecting the nation's harvests.

After seven bountiful years, the famine arose and covered the entire region, including the land of Israel. Jacob sent his sons into Canaan to buy food. There they encountered Joseph, whom they hadn't seen for twenty years. He forgave them and told them to bring their aged father to Canaan for the rest of the famine years. Pharaoh gave the Israelites a portion of land in Goshen—the most fertile part of Egypt.

The Israelites stayed in Egypt. After Pharaoh's death the new king began to fear the growing number of the Israelites and eventually enslaved them. They remained in Egypt 430 years until the time of Moses.

3. *From Moses to King Saul.* The Bible moves its spotlight to Moses (about 1526–1406 B.C.).

God chose Moses to lead the people out of slavery and back into the Promised Land—the land of Canaan that

God had once given to Abraham. Pharaoh refused to free them, and Moses worked miracles, including the sending of ten plagues across the land. The last plague took the life of the firstborn son of every family that didn't kill a lamb and sprinkle its blood on the lintel of the door. If they spread the blood, the Bible says the angel of death saw it and passed over (hence, the term *Passover*) and didn't kill the firstborn son.

The death plague forced Pharaoh to give in, and he sent the Israelites away. Yet almost as soon as they had gone, Pharaoh changed his mind and sent his army to bring the Israelites back.

God led the Israelites to the Red Sea, parted the waters, and led them across on dry ground. The pursuing Egyptians were drowned when the waters returned to their normal level.

Moses led the people from the Red Sea to Mount Sinai. On the way, God miraculously provided food. At Mount Sinai, through Moses, God revealed the laws and social plans that would mold the Israelites into a holy nation. The laws, which included the Ten Commandments, are often referred to as the Mosaic Law. They became the binding laws for Israelites and continue today.

From Sinai, God led the Israelites to Kadesh, where Moses sent twelve spies into Canaan. All twelve agreed the land was rich and fertile but full of giants; however, ten of them wanted to go back to Egypt. Only Caleb and Joshua believed that, with God's help, they could defeat the people.

The Israelites accepted the fear-driven advice of the majority and turned away from Canaan. For their lack of faith, God condemned the people to wander until the last of those who left Egypt at age twenty or older had died. That process took about forty years.

Moses also wasn't allowed to enter the Promised Land because he had rebelled against God at Meribah (see Num. 20:10–20).

At the end of their years of wandering, Moses spoke to the congregated people for the last time and turned over his leadership to Joshua. After Moses gave his farewell to the Israelites, he died on Mount Nebo.

Joshua led Israel into Canaan. Just as at the Red Sea, God divided the overflowing Jordan River so they could cross over on dry land. At Jericho, the first battle they fought, the soldiers marched around the walled city for seven days. On the last day the people blew trumpets, and the walls of the city fell down.

Israel conquered the entire country. Then Joshua divided the land by lot among the Israelite tribes. During Joshua's lifetime, the people stayed faithful to God's laws.

After Joshua's death, people turned away from God until "everyone did as he saw fit" (Judg. 21:25). The leaders, called judges, for the next period were military heroes, outcasts, and even a woman named Deborah. Samuel, who next dominated the scene, stands as the last of the judges and first of the prophets.

The people demanded a king instead of judges. At God's direction, Samuel anointed Saul as Israel's first king.

4. *The United Kingdom.* During his early reign, Saul obeyed God. Over the years, however, he changed. For instance, his jealous anger turned against David, a young

warrior who had killed the giant Goliath. Out of jealousy, Saul tried to murder David.

God chose David to be the next king, and he promised the kingship to David's family forever. Saul ruled forty years. After his death, David became king and made Jerusalem the spiritual and political center of the nation.

David's son Solomon was the next king. In spite of Solomon's legendary wisdom, he didn't always live wisely. He carried out David's political plan and strengthened his hold on the territories conquered by his father. He was also a shrewd businessman, and he made trade agreements that brought vast wealth to Israel. His lavish style of living, however, increased the burden of taxes upon the common people.

5. *The Divided Kingdom.* After Solomon died, Israel stumbled into civil war. Rehoboam succeeded his father Solomon, and Jeroboam led ten of the twelve tribes in a rebellion to form a separate kingdom called Israel. The Bible also calls it Samaria (which was its capital), and we often refer to it as the Northern Kingdom.

None of Israel's kings served God, and the Southern Kingdom, called Judah or Jerusalem, had a poor record, and the nation went downward spiritually. Asa, Azariah, Jehoshaphat, Jotham, Joash (Jehoash), Hezekiah, Amaziah, and Josiah were the only faithful kings, and none of them matched the zeal and commitment of David.

Two important prophets emerged in Israel during the divided monarchy. The first was Elijah, who opposed King Ahab and Queen Jezebel. He performed a number of miracles and was the faithful voice for God. The second prophet, Elisha, was Elijah's protégé. There are more miracles recorded in the stories of those two leaders than of anyone else in the Old Testament.

Other prophets spoke and wrote during the time of the divided monarchy, including Isaiah, Jeremiah, Amos, Hosea, and Micah.

Because of Israel's continued disobedience, the prophets warned that they would be conquered and taken away from the land. God also promised they would return to the land. The nation of Assyria conquered the Northern Kingdom (about 722 B.C.). In 587–586 B.C. Babylon destroyed Jerusalem and carried many of the people of the Southern Kingdom into exile.

6. *The Exile to the Return.* As God had promised, the Jews returned from exile in Babylon. They came back between 536 and 525 B.C., led by Ezra and Nehemiah, who rebuilt Jerusalem and reestablished worship. Those two men demanded faithful obedience to God. The writing prophets Zechariah and Haggai encouraged the people in their work. Toward the end of the period, Malachi condemned them for slipping back into their sinful ways.

Between the Old and New Testaments

It's not always clear what happened during the four hundred years between the writing of Malachi and the time Jesus was born. We call this the intertestamental period because it is the time between the writings of the Old Testament and New Testament.

The restored nation of Israel had serious political upsets. After Alexander the Great conquered the Persian Empire, Greek princes and generals wrestled for the right to govern what is now called the Middle East. The

Seleucid King Antiochus III took Canaan away from Egypt in 198 B.C. and tried to make it a base for building a new empire in the East. Antiochus III was no match for the Roman legions, and they defeated his army in 190 B.C. and made him a puppet ruler.

The family of Jewish priests, the Maccabees, began a civil war against the Seleucid governors and captured Jerusalem in 164 B.C. They weren't able to push the Seleucids completely out of their affairs until 134 B.C. In that year, John Hyrcanus I of the Maccabee family set up his own dynasty, known as the Hasmoneans. They ruled until 37 B.C., when Rome established the Herodian family as the new puppet government.

The books of 1 and 2 Maccabees describe the Maccabean revolt and the chaos in Israel up until the time of the Hasmoneans. Roman Catholics include these books and other writings from the intertestamental period in their Bible, but Protestants do not, although translations of them are sometimes included in Protestant versions of the Bible.

The New Testament

1. *The Life of Jesus Christ.* The New Testament introduces the Messiah, Jesus Christ, and the beginning of the Christian church. The writings of Matthew, Mark, Luke, and John tell most of what we know about Jesus. The four Gospel writers portrayed the person and ministry of Jesus by recording what he did and said. Each writer presents a slightly different viewpoint.

The birth and infancy of Jesus Christ with the details, such as the Virgin Mary (the mother of Jesus), Joseph and

Mary's trip to Bethlehem, the birth of the baby Jesus in Bethlehem, and the angels who announced his birth to the shepherds, are told only in Matthew and Luke.

After Jesus was born, his parents dedicated him at the temple in Jerusalem (Luke 2:22–28). King Herod wanted to be certain that the people did not rally around the infant king to start a rebellion, so he ordered his soldiers to kill all the male babies in Bethlehem (Matt. 2:16). Jesus' family fled into Egypt to escape the evil decree. After Herod died, they returned to Israel and settled in the town of Nazareth.

The Bible says little about Jesus until his public ministry. It began by his being baptized by John the Baptist. A voice from heaven said, "This is my Son, whom I love; with him I am well pleased" (Matt. 3:17). Then the Holy Spirit led Jesus into the wilderness to be tempted by the Devil for forty days.

After the temptation, Jesus began his public ministry. He

- went into private homes,
- sat at public feasts,
- taught the common people,
- worshiped with other Jews in the synagogues,
- denounced hypocrisy and taught the true path to God, and
- performed miracles and healings.

Most of the religious leaders failed to accept Jesus as the Messiah, although the people listened and many proclaimed him the Messiah.

Judas Iscariot, one of the twelve disciples, betrayed Jesus to the hostile leaders of Jerusalem. After a mock trial, the Romans nailed Jesus to a cross to die with a convicted criminal on either side of him.

Three days after his death by crucifixion, Jesus rose from the grave and appeared to many of his followers. He also gave final instructions to his disciples to go into all the world with the gospel.

As the disciples watched Jesus ascend into heaven, two angels appeared and promised that Jesus would return.

2. *The Ministry of the Apostles.* The message of salvation through Jesus Christ spread from Jerusalem to Rome—the center of the Western world. Here are two ways to see the story as told in the Book of Acts.

The church was born at Jerusalem. The message of salvation spread from Jerusalem to Judea and then to Samaria. From there, the gospel went all over Asia Minor and Eastern Europe. The Book of Acts ends when the gospel reaches Rome, where it would then spread into the rest of the world.

Peter was the great leader of the apostles, and his ministry guided the enthusiasm of the early church (Acts 1–11).

The second stage of the church's growth began with persecution of the church in Jerusalem and the conversion of Saul, who became known as the apostle Paul. His leadership dominates the rest of Acts as he is the central character in the expansion of the church. Although the door to Gentiles opened through the ministry of Peter, it was Paul who led the church toward a total integration of all people.

Bible history, which describes the ministry of the early church, ends with Paul imprisoned in Rome. He lived for two years in a rented house, continuing to preach to the people who visited him.

CHAPTER 22

Twelve Commands of God

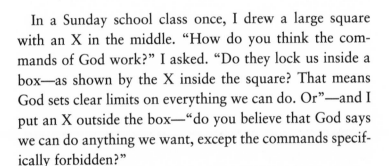

In a Sunday school class once, I drew a large square with an X in the middle. "How do you think the commands of God work?" I asked. "Do they lock us inside a box—as shown by the X inside the square? That means God sets clear limits on everything we can do. Or"—and I put an X outside the box—"do you believe that God says we can do anything we want, except the commands specifically forbidden?"

We had a lively discussion in that class of thirty people. I wanted them to think about God's purpose in giving laws to humans, specifically the Ten Commandments. Were they given, as some believed, to keep us hemmed in so we would follow God? Or were they simply a way of saying that God has given us a world and a life to enjoy, which is restricted by only a few rules?

Through the centuries, this has been debated in a variety of ways, and usually not so simplistically.

Christian thinkers have always maintained that the Ten Commandments occupy a special place, although what that special place is has caused differences. Basically, we've had two positions. First, of course, is that they are as binding on us as they were on Israel. The second says, "No, Jesus' death fulfilled the law. Hence, we have no demands on us, except those of the New Testament."

Let's look at those commandments. In Hebrew, the Ten Commandments are called Ten Words, and scholars sometimes refer to them as the Decalogue, which also means "Ten Words."

These commands are given in their entirety twice in the Old Testament with only slight variations. The one we usually refer to is in Exodus 20:1–17. At Mount Sinai, Moses brought the law to the people on two tablets of stone. They are repeated in Deuteronomy 5:6–21, just before the Israelites traveled into the Promised Land.

Most likely, God intended for the Israelites to memorize the Ten Commandments and then for the entire community to receive them together. As many people have pointed out, not only is the number of commands the same as the number of fingers, but there's also a similarity of form. Most common, of course, is "You shall not" followed by a verb. Placed at the beginning of a lengthy block of legal materials, the Ten Words functioned as a summary of the covenant between God and Israel at public occasions of national reaffirmation of loyalty to Yahweh, much as we Americans repeat the Pledge of Allegiance today.

The Ten Commandments

In earlier versions, the translators used "thou," which pointed to individuals as part of the wider community. The modern use of "you" (which can be singular or plural in

English) obscures the fact that God strikes the individual heart with these words before they apply to the whole community.

There is a slight difference in numbering these laws. The commandment counted as the first by most Christians, "You shall have no other gods before me" (Exod. 20:3), is considered the first half of the second commandment in Jewish tradition. Lutherans and Roman Catholics combine this command with the prohibition against graven images to form the first. Exodus 20:17 is then divided into two commandments to make up the ten.

This is the way most Protestants know the Ten Commandments from Exodus 20 (for the other version, see Deut. 5:6–21).

1. *"You shall have no other gods before me"* (Exod. 20:3). The first commandment doesn't deny or debate the existence of other gods or powers—after all, the Israelites had just come out of a country that worshiped many gods. Some of the original hearers may have carried the idea of a plurality of gods with them. This first statement demands total allegiance to Yahweh, the covenant giver.

2. *"You shall not make for yourself an idol in the form of anything in heaven above or on the earth beneath or in the waters below"* (Exod. 20:4). The prohibition against graven images may have been to stop Israel from making images of Yahweh. The reason is because God can't be localized in an object such as a golden calf (see Exod. 20:4–6). To permit this would symbolically make God an object of manipulation. God has images in the world, but they walk on two feet; they love Yahweh and keep the commandments (see Gen. 1:26).

When people crafted images, they didn't strictly worship them. They considered that they had some element of the deity present within the image. Often the form of the image represented an outstanding quality of that deity.

To interpret it for today, this commandment denies that we can insure the presence of God by any action of our own. God is so far beyond human understanding that any effort to make anything to represent Yahweh is futile, inadequate, and reduces God to mere human understanding. Is it any wonder that the first petition in the Lord's Prayer reads, "Hallowed be your name" (Matt. 6:9b)?

3. *"You shall not misuse the name of the* LORD *your God"* (Exod. 20:7). This command is aimed at those who invoke the name of God for trivial uses. For example, some people invoked the name of Yahweh (or Jesus today) as a kind of magical guarantee of an answer, regardless of the request. It's also a way of saying that if we are godly, we don't need to swear or pledge God's name to make others believe our words.

There is also the use of profanity—which shows a lack of respect for God and the inability of the speakers to control their tongues.

4. *"Remember the Sabbath day by keeping it holy"* (Exod. 20:8). This is the most controversial command—and the one that few Christians make any attempt to observe strictly, even those who believe we are bound by these commands.

This is the command to rest on the Sabbath. In the act of creation, God worked six days and ceased on the seventh. In Deuteronomy 5:12–15, the Sabbath is mentioned as a day of remembrance of liberation from Egyptian slavery. The command to set apart one day ("keep it holy") stands against endless self-destructive human greed. It wasn't intended, as some have tried to impose, to be a day of worship, but as a day to cease from work and to enjoy life.

Two motivations are given to cease from our work. (1) It is freedom from slavery—a way not to become enslaved by the demands of this life. (2) It is God's design from the beginning of creation. Genesis 2:2–3 says that God kept *shabbat*—which comes from a Hebrew word that means "to desist," not to rest.

5. *"Honor your father and your mother, so that you may live long in the land the* LORD *your God is giving you"* (Exod. 20:12). This is the only one of the Ten Commandments accompanied with a promise. "Honoring" implied caring for parents, that is, for the young to provide for the elderly. This is beyond a picture of our early training for children. In the Bible, the family is the foundation of society. Parents care for children, and after the children are grown, they care for their parents.

6. *"You shall not murder"* (Exod. 20:13). Although older translations read, "Thou shalt not kill," the intention here is not to murder out of hatred or self-interest. Life is a gift from God and to take another's life unlawfully stands at the head of the Old Testament list of sins. (To take the life of enemies in war was never considered murder.)

7. *"You shall not commit adultery"* (Exod. 20:14). This command guards married and family values against the intrusion of third parties.

8. *"You shall not steal"* (Exod. 20:15). This command protects private property. By taking others' possessions,

we accuse the divine one of inadequately providing for our needs. It's also a sin against others. For us today, it's clear proof that we don't love our neighbors as ourselves. If we did, we wouldn't steal from them.

9. *"You shall not give false testimony against your neighbor"* (Exod. 20:16). This is clearer than the older versions against bearing false witness. This command isn't so much against lying in general, because it refers to perjury in court. Such actions threaten the survival of a community because the weak, the disadvantaged, and the falsely accused had no recourse before judges. To bear witness was a public duty (see Lev. 5:1). At a time when the death penalty was common, giving false evidence could be equivalent to committing murder because the testimony condemned the innocent (see Deut. 19:16, 18–19).

10. *"You shall not covet your neighbor's house . . . wife . . . his manservant or maidservant, his ox or donkey, or anything that belongs to your neighbor"* (Exod. 20:17). This command against covetousness points beyond the public acts and duties to private attitudes. This is an attitude, a mind-set, and an action "in rehearsal." That is, covetousness begins in the mind and the desires. We dwell on it, rehearse it, and then do the deed. The prohibition implies that a wrong attitude will lead to an action against another. This tenth command is unenforceable, but it strikes at the inordinate desire that leads to conspiracies of illegal, ruthless crimes.

In many places, the word translated *covet* means no more than "desire" or "lust" as in Romans 7:7. This lies at the heart of the sin of social dissatisfaction. If we pray, "give us this day our daily bread," we have no right to be dissatisfied with our heavenly Father's provisions.

The Other Two Commands

In the New Testament, a Pharisee (a Jewish religious leader) tried to trick Jesus by asking him which was the greatest commandment of the law.

Rather than choosing one of the Ten Commandments, Jesus quoted Deuteronomy 6:5, which said to love God with the total being. Jesus didn't stop with that verse. He went on to say that there was an equally important second command ("The second is like it," Matt. 22:39). This time he quoted Leviticus 19:18, "Love your neighbor as yourself." He continued, "All the Law and the Prophets hang on these two commandments" (Matt. 22:40).

In that encounter, Jesus laid down the complete definition of Christian faith. First, the Christian religion consists of loving God. The verse he quoted is part of the Shema, the basic creed of Judaism, and the one sentence that Jewish children commit to memory. "Hear, O Israel: the LORD our God, the LORD is one. Love the LORD your God with all your heart and with all your soul and with all your strength" (Deut. 6:4–5). The statement means that God demands our total love—a commitment that dominates our emotions, directs our thoughts, and motivates our actions.

The second command Jesus linked with it refers to our love for others. This is really the proof of the first. The only way we can prove that we love God is by the way we treat other people. The order is essential—not in terms of time but importance and emphasis. We first love God—

that's our motivator—and that's how we learn to love other human beings.

To be a true follower means to love God and to love other people, not with a kind of sentimentality, but with a commitment. One more thing: The love God commands isn't an emotion; it's an act of the will.

CHAPTER 23

God's Other Laws

Why have laws? The simple answer is that we need them. Without laws, people take advantage of one another. The Book of Judges ends with the statement that all the people did what was right in their own understanding—and they didn't consider the needs of other people.

We also need laws because we're all natural lawbreakers. And we need just laws to maintain quality life within a community.

Before the people of Israel went into the Promised Land, Moses read them God's laws, which included much more than the Ten Commandments. In fact, looking at all the laws listed in Exodus, Leviticus, Numbers, and Deuteronomy makes it obvious that laws regulated daily lives. They included everything from the food they ate to the way they treated foreigners. The laws weren't meant to enslave but to make life easier and to benefit the entire community.

God delivered a band of slaves from Egypt and set them up as a new nation. Giving them the law through Moses became the decisive moment in their history. It was the formation of the covenant between God and Israel, and it became the foundation for all future Israelite law.

When Christians or Jews say "the law," they probably refer to the rules and regulations of the Old Testament, the unique law code given as direct revelation to Israel. Too often, however, Christians consider the Old Testament as a book of heavy laws and the New Testament as a book of grace. This isn't true. Divine grace and mercy are the foundation of the laws in the Old Testament. The grace shown in the New Testament grew out of the laws of the Old Testament.

Law and Covenant

Israelite law is covenant law. That is, the law rests on an understanding of the meaning of life within the community. The meaning of their life was provided by the saving action of God. Yahweh saved the people and had a purpose for them. Through Israel, all families of the earth were to be blessed (Gen. 12:3). The covenant relationship issues in a distinctive type of Israelite law that is of fundamental importance—and it set forth the policy on the basis of which they understood all law.

Israel wasn't the only nation to have a law code in the ancient world; however, the other codes that existed when the Israelites went into the Promised Land were different. Those laws usually said that the gods had given the king the power to reign. A long section that extolled the king's worthiness to reign followed this. Then came the king's laws grouped by subject, and the law code ended with a series of blessings for obedience and curses for disobedience.

The Law of the Old Testament, often referred to as the Mosaic Law, was different in many ways. First, although peoples of the ancient world believed their laws originated with the gods, those laws were very subjective and personal in the way they were applied. The law was decided on a case-by-case basis and at the king's discretion. Even the gods were under the law and could suffer punishment for violation—unless they were powerful enough to conquer the punishers. The king ruled for the gods from their temple. Although the human ruler didn't live under a written law code, he had a personal relationship with the divinities.

By contrast, the biblical law came from Yahweh, the one who is holy, righteous, and good. For Israel, God was the great king who issued the laws and made them binding on the people. God was also the one who upheld the law. Perhaps even more significant, the laws of Israel were universal and not based on whim, preferences, or human prejudice.

Here is one of the great expressions of God's words for Moses to pass on to the people: "Now if you obey me fully and keep my covenant, then out of all nations you will be my treasured possession. Although the whole earth is mine, you will be for me a kingdom of priests and a holy nation" (Exod. 19:5–6).

Underlying Principles

The principles behind the laws of the Bible, in marked contrast to those behind other laws of that culture, are based on the revealed character and purpose of God. They also point toward God's goal—the salvation of humanity. They show divine protection for each person's integrity and reflect the understanding that God made human beings the stewards of the earth.

Another way to see this is to contrast them with the Code of Hammurabi. That ancient code, for example, preserves three separate social classes, and it legally degraded the lower class and protected the position of those at the top of society. Biblical law sees all people as creatures of God, equal to one another.

Here are some of the underlying principles of God's laws.

1. *Basic to the idea of God's laws is this: Every crime—no matter how minor—is a crime against God.* When individuals offend society, they offend God. As the supreme judge, God disciplines those who violate the commandments. The nation is responsible to uphold the law and to make certain that justice prevails.

2. *All human life is valuable, because humanity was created in the image of God.* Consequently, biblical law was more humane than the laws in other societies. It avoided bodily mutilation and savage punishments.

For example, when we read "eye for eye" (Exod. 21:24), this didn't command anyone to put out another's eye. It prohibited an angry person doing more. If one man put out a person's eye, *the most* retaliation the victim could expect to enact was to blind one eye of the aggressor.

If those from a higher social class injured people of lower social status, they were not excused by the mere payment of a fine. The only equivalent of human life was human life itself.

Centuries before the law, God said to Noah after the flood, "Any person who murders must be killed. Yes, you must execute anyone who murders another person, for to kill a person is to kill a living being made in God's image" (Gen. 9:5–6 NLT).

3. *Everyone is equal before God.* In some pagan cultures, the rich often bought their way out of punishment, but the Mosaic Law said that all criminals had to pay for their own crimes (Num. 35:31).

Something quite revolutionary was that God's law especially protects the orphans, widows, slaves, and strangers from injustice (see Exod. 21:20–21; 22:21–23). These people were the defenseless—the ones least able to stand up for themselves—but they weren't beyond the compassion of God.

People weren't to receive handouts but were expected to work for their own living. Israelites, however, were to care for those who were unable to care for themselves, such as the widows and orphans.

4. *The law is to bring people to total submission to God.* God's laws show divine care about every aspect of life. It wasn't enough to offer formal worship or moral behavior. Everything they had came from God, so they were to serve with their whole being.

God enforced the law when human agents wouldn't and punished Israel by applying the law fairly. The people were taught that God was present as judge at every court trial, no matter what verdict the human judge rendered.

5. *The law is a national responsibility.* God's law isn't the private property of the upper class. All Jews knew the law and the penalty for breaking it. At times, the whole community punished the lawbreaker because all of the people had to uphold the law.

Judges represented God, but they also represented the law-abiding community. Cases of murder required evidence from two or three witnesses, and the verdict was announced publicly at the city gate. If the person was found guilty, the witnesses themselves executed the murderer, or the victim's next of kin or the whole community participated.

6. *The law is also an individual responsibility.* The Bible stressed that personal duty to God is more important than the responsibility to adhere to community policies. Even when their neighbors and friends did wrong, God still held them individually responsible for their own actions.

7. *Biblical laws call for humane treatment of the poor and helpless, as well as kindness toward animals.* This was a revolutionary concept. The law said that every animal is useful, and the Israelites were to feed each animal according to the work it did. They weren't allowed to beat or treat animals with cruelty. Even the animals were to cease from working on the Sabbath.

Practical Applications

Here are a few examples of the Old Testament put into practice:

- When Israelites observed beasts carrying loads too heavy for them—even if the animals belonged to neighbors—they were to take part of the burden themselves.

- If an Israelite borrowed a coat or other important item, it had to be returned at nightfall.
- When people couldn't earn a living on their own, they could go into voluntary servitude by signing a contract to become servants. However, their masters had to treat them kindly.
- The freeborn couldn't be kidnapped and sold into slavery.
- Creditors couldn't enter into another's house to collect an unpaid debt. (The law honored the right of the creditor, but it also guarded the rights of the debtor.)
- Travelers and foreigners could enter a field and gather food to eat, but they couldn't carry off any.
- Farmers were to leave gleanings in the field for wild animals as well as the poor.
- Farmers paid wages to hired hands every day because the poor needed the money to buy their food.
- When Israelites loaned money, they were not to charge interest.

∞

By the time of Jesus, a thousand years after Moses, the law had become highly diversified, with different groups interpreting the Old Testament to advance their own purposes. Too often that went far beyond the interpretation of specific passages and sometimes caused them to disagree with other teachers. All the groups relied on an oral law— the handed-down interpretation of scribes, teachers, and priests through the centuries. Those oral traditions, rather than the written Law of Moses, eventually regulated the details of everyday life.

Those teachings were not part of the law given to Moses but understandings and interpretations through the centuries that took on the meaning of law. In some instances, the interpretations became ways to circumvent or deny what God had actually said.

Jesus spoke to an unsophisticated audience. His goal wasn't to interpret the law and set himself up as a teacher who opposed the others. Jesus opposed any style of interpretation that removed or denied God's original intentions. He wanted to destroy the encrustations of tradition and point the people back to God's intentions in the law itself.

CHAPTER 24

A Few of God's Friends

The Bible is filled with stories about people, especially the people of faith. When we say Shadrach and Meshach, most of us immediately add Abed-nego, and we're already recalling the story of the three young men and the fiery furnace. What image does Noah bring? Mary Magdalene? Peter? Ruth?

Biblical literacy revolves around people—and here are some of the significant and good individuals whose names appear within the pages of the holy Book.

Aaron. The older brother of Moses, he was first high priest of the Hebrew nation.

Abel. He was the second son of Adam and Eve. His older brother Cain, who was a farmer, brought an offering to God, but God "looked with favor on Abel and his offering" (Gen. 4:4), rather than on Cain and his offering. Envious of Abel, Cain killed his brother and was cursed by God.

Abed-nego: One of three Hebrew young men whom King Nebuchadnezzar had thrown into a fiery furnace for refusing to bow down and worship a golden image. God miraculously protected all three of them (see Dan. 3:12–30).

Abraham. The first great patriarch of ancient Israel and a primary model of faithfulness for Christianity. The accounts about Abraham occur in Genesis 11:26–25:11.

Adam. The first human, created by God on the sixth day of creation, he was placed in the Garden of Eden. God gave him and his mate Eve dominion over the fields and the animals and told them, "Be fruitful and increase" (Gen. 1:28). He and his wife disobeyed God's command by eating from a forbidden tree. They were cast out of the garden and later died.

Andrew. He was the brother of Simon Peter and one of Jesus' first disciples. Both Andrew and Peter were fishermen. All lists of the disciples place Andrew among the first four (see Matt. 10:2–4; Mark 3:16–19; Luke 6:14–16; Acts 1:13). Tradition says Andrew's field of labor was the region north of the Black Sea. He became the patron saint of Scotland. Tradition also says that Andrew was martyred in Achaia (Greece) by crucifixion on an X-shaped cross.

Barnabas. Originally known as Joseph, he was a Levite from Cyprus who sold his land and gave the money to the church in Jerusalem. Later, Barnabas became an apostle in the early church (Acts 4:36–37; 11:19–26) and Paul's companion on his first missionary journey (Acts 13:1–15:41).

Benjamin. He was Jacob's twelfth son and was born to Rachel, the favored wife (Gen. 35:18, 24).

Caleb. One of the twelve spies sent by Moses to investigate the land of Canaan (see Num. 13:6–12). Only he and Joshua brought in a good report and believed they could conquer the land. Because of their faithfulness, those two were the only adults who left Egypt and who entered the Promised Land.

Cornelius. A Roman centurion stationed at Caesarea, he was sympathetic to the Jewish faith. After having a vision, he sent for Peter, who explained to him about faith in Jesus Christ. He believed and was baptized along with his household (Acts 10). This is the first recorded New Testament conversion of a non-Jew.

Cyrus. Cyrus the Great founded and ruled the Persian Empire (558–529 B.C.). He conquered Babylon in 539 B.C. and proclaimed that the exiled Jews could return to Jerusalem to rebuild their temple. Isaiah called him God's shepherd and the Lord's anointed servant (see Isa. 44:28; 45:1).

Daniel. A member of the exiled Jewish community, Daniel was promoted within the courts of Babylon. He was a prophet and interpreter of Nebuchadnezzar's dreams. He is credited with writing the Old Testament book that bears his name.

David. Only one David appears in the Bible—and we read that name more than one thousand times. David was a shepherd, a skillful musician, and a valiant man of war. While only a teenager, he killed the Philistine giant Goliath with a stone from his sling. He was the ideal king and succeeded Saul, Israel's first king.

David reigned for thirty-three years over all Israel. He broke the power of the Philistines, united the nation, and made Jerusalem the religious center of the nation. Mary, the mother of Jesus, was a direct descendent of David.

Deborah. The only woman judge mentioned was also a prophetess. She summoned Barak to gather the tribes to attack Sisera by the Kishon River. They won a great victory for Israel.

Elijah. The stormy prophet of Israel in the ninth century B.C. rebuked King Ahab and his wife Jezebel. He challenged the people of the Northern Kingdom to reject Baal worship and to return to the true God.

Enoch. Although three men are named Enoch in the Bible, the important one was the father of Methuselah. After living 365 years, Enoch "walked with God; then he was no more, because God took him away" (Gen. 5:24). Many believe this means he was "translated" into God's presence without experiencing death.

Esther. She was chosen by Ahasuerus to be his queen over Persia. The Book of Esther tells the story of her delivering the Jews from certain death by the wicked Haman.

Ezra. A priest and a scribe in exile in Babylon during the reign of Artaxerxes, king of Persia, he returned to Jerusalem with gifts from the king for the exiled Jews. Once the temple was built, the people gathered to hear Ezra read from the book of the law from early morning until midday. Ezra ordered the Jews who had foreign wives to put them and their children away. Through his reforms, Ezra turned Israel back to serving God.

Hezekiah. One of the few kings of Judah who did right in God's sight was Hezekiah. He destroyed pagan worship and brought about some reform (716–687 B.C) to turn the people back to Yahweh.

Isaac. The only son of Abraham by his wife Sarah, he became the father of Jacob and Esau. God had promised to make Abraham's descendants a great nation that would become God's chosen people. But the promised son was a long time in coming. Twenty-five years after God first promised a son, Isaac was born. Abraham was then one hundred years old, and Sarah was ninety.

Isaiah. The greatest of the Old Testament prophets, he has the most predictions about the coming Messiah. He is the author of the book that bears his name. Tradition says that Isaiah's ministry extended from about 740 B.C. until at least 701 and that he died by being sawed in half during the reign of the evil King Manasseh of Judah.

Jacob (also called *Israel*). The grandson of Abraham, Jacob was the younger child of Isaac and Rebekah and the twin of Esau. A crafty, skillful, intelligent, and self-reliant man, he deceived his father and stole the birthright from Esau. He was the father of the twelve sons who became the leaders of Israel's twelve tribes. While never denying his record, the Bible holds him up as a man who believed God.

James. Three men have the name of James in the New Testament.

1. *A Galilean fisherman, son of Zebedee, and brother of John.* He was one of the twelve disciples of Jesus. His name always appears with John. James, along with John and Peter, made up Jesus' inner circle of disciples.

2. *The son of Alphaeus, another of Jesus' disciples.* We know nothing more about him.

3. *Jesus' brother.* He is mentioned in the Gospels (Matt. 13:55). He appears in Acts and in the writings of Paul as an important leader of the early church, possibly the pastor in Jerusalem.

Jeremiah. The prophet who wrote the book bearing his name lived during the seventh century B.C. He prophesied during the reign of King Josiah and until the fall of Jerusalem. He is often thought of as the weeping prophet. Among his tortures, Jeremiah was beaten, thrown in a pit, and put into stocks. When the Babylonians overthrew Jerusalem, Nebuchadnezzar gave special orders to care for the prophet. Tradition says Jeremiah died in Babylon.

Joash. He was one of the better kings of Judah. When his grandmother, Queen Athaliah, took over the throne of Judah, the Southern Kingdom, she killed the family of her late son, King Ahaziah. The priest Jehoiada hid the infant Joash in the temple until the boy was seven. Jehoiada then proclaimed him king, and the loyal guard killed Athaliah. Joash (under the priest's influence) immediately brought reform to the land. He repaired the temple with freewill offerings and routed out pagan ways.

Job. In spite of his physical and spiritual suffering, this Old Testament man is noted for his faith in God. The Book of Job is a lengthy, poetic narrative consisting mostly of Job's discussions about God and the divine ways with his friends, Eliphaz, Bildad, Zophar, and Elihu.

John. The son of Zebedee, the brother of James, and a Galilean fisherman, he was one of the first disciples Jesus chose. He is identified as the writer of the Gospel of John, three short letters, and the Book of Revelation. He is also identified as the disciple whom Jesus loved—a phrase referring to his relationship as Jesus' special friend.

John the Baptist. The son of Elizabeth and Zacharias, he was also Jesus' cousin. He behaved and dressed much like Elijah the prophet, and Jesus compared him to that prophet, calling him the fulfillment of the promise of Elijah to come again. John preached a baptism of repentance for the forgiveness of sin. He also baptized Jesus. Later he was beheaded as a favor to the daughter of Herodias.

Jonah. A great fish swallowed the prophet before he finally obeyed God's command to preach repentance to the Assyrian city of Nineveh. He is likely the same prophet who predicted the remarkable expansion of Israel's territory during the reign of Jeroboam II (about 793–753 B.C., 2 Kings 14:25).

Joseph. The Bible lists six significant men named Joseph.

1. *The son of Jacob and Rachel.* He was his father's favorite son. Joseph is the central figure in Genesis 37–50. His jealous brothers sold him into slavery. His buyers took him to Egypt, where he eventually triumphed as Pharaoh's right-hand man. Later he reunited with his family and arranged for all of them to live in Egypt during the years of famine. The Book of Genesis ends with the death of Joseph.

2. *The husband of Mary who was Jesus' mother.* Matthew describes him as a son of David. He was a carpenter in Nazareth who went with his wife to Bethlehem for a census count. Jesus was born in Bethlehem during their visit to the city.

3. *The brother of Jesus.*

4. *A man from Arimathea, a wealthy member of the Jewish council.* Joseph remained a secret disciple of Jesus until the crucifixion, when he asked Pilate for the body of

Jesus. After Pilate agreed, Joseph had Jesus' body laid in the tomb he had prepared for his own burial.

5. *Apostle-in-nomination*. He and Matthias became candidates to take the place of Judas Iscariot among the Twelve. The lot fell on Matthias.

6. *Called Barnabas*. (See *Barnabas*.) He accompanied Paul during much of his ministry.

Joshua. This is the same root word for Jesus, which means "Savior." He was Moses' faithful assistant and his successor. The book bearing his name tells of his leading the people into the Promised Land. Under his leadership, the twelve tribes divided the land and conquered their enemies.

Lazarus. The New Testament mentions two men by this name.

1. *Brother of Mary and Martha of Bethany*. When he died, Jesus raised Lazarus back to life after four days.

2. *A beggar*. His name appears in Jesus' parable about a rich man and a poor man—the only time a person is named in a parable (Luke 16:19–31).

Luke. Called the beloved physician, he wrote the third Gospel and Acts. Likely a Gentile, he traveled with the apostle Paul. The "we" sections of Acts indicate that he traveled with Paul on his second and third missionary journeys and his trip to Rome.

Mark, John. An associate of Peter and Paul, he probably authored the second Gospel. Mark's lasting impact on the Christian church comes from his writing rather than his life. He was the first to develop the literary form known as the Gospel. His mother Mary was an influential woman of Jerusalem.

Mary. The New Testament lists six Marys:

1. *The mother of Jesus.* The Gospels contain little information about her. She was a virgin, a kinswoman of Elizabeth, who was the mother of John the Baptist. The last mention of her is that she prayed in the upper room with the disciples before the coming of the Holy Spirit.

2. *Mary Magdalene, named for Magdala, a town on the Sea of Galilee.* One of the women who followed Jesus from Galilee, she also witnessed the crucifixion of Jesus and was the first person to go to the empty tomb on Sunday morning to anoint Jesus' body.

3. *Mary, the mother of James (the younger) and Joses, the disciples of Jesus.* One of the women who followed Jesus and ministered to him, she was present at the crucifixion and at the tomb early on the morning of the resurrection.

4. *Mary, the wife of Clopas.* We know only that she was among the women at the cross when Jesus died.

5. *Mary of Bethany, the sister of Martha and Lazarus.* She sat at Jesus' feet and listened while her sister fretted. Jesus praised Mary for her devotion to him. Jesus raised her brother Lazarus from the dead.

6. *Mary, the mother of John Mark.* In her house in Jerusalem Christians met for prayer.

Matthew. One of the twelve apostles of Jesus, he is also known as Levi. Before he followed Jesus, Matthew was a tax collector. He was the author of the first Gospel.

Melchizedek. The priest-king of Salem met Abraham and blessed the patriarch. His name came to symbolize the ideal priesthood (Gen. 14:18; Ps. 110:4; Heb. 7:1–21).

Meshach. Along with Shadrach and Abed-nego, he refused to bow down and worship a pagan image in Babylon. All three were cast into a burning furnace, but God delivered them and they were unhurt.

Methuselah. He became the father of Lamech at age 187 and lived a total of 969 years—the oldest recorded life in the Bible.

Miriam. She was the sister of Moses and Aaron. She watched over the infant Moses when he was laid in the reed basket, and she summoned a nurse from among the Hebrew women when Pharaoh's daughter found the baby and adopted him. After the deliverance from Egypt, Miriam led in a victorious dance and song.

Moses. The Hebrew prophet, leader, and lawgiver delivered the Israelites from Egyptian slavery. He led the former slaves during their forty years of wanderings in the wilderness. From a race of oppressed slaves, Moses built a nation and instructed them on how to follow God's laws.

Nehemiah. He was a cupbearer to Artaxerxes I, king of Persia. After learning that the walls of Jerusalem were broken down and its gates destroyed, he asked the king for permission to rebuild. Artaxerxes appointed him governor, supplied him with building materials, and sent him to Jerusalem. The Book of Nehemiah tells of his organizing and rebuilding. Despite local opposition, he and his followers completed rebuilding the city walls.

Nicodemus. This Pharisee and a member of the Sanhedrin (Jewish council) became a disciple of Jesus. Jesus pointed out to him the need to be born from above (or again) in order to enter the kingdom of heaven (see John 3:1–21).

Noah. He is the hero of the flood story. God instructed him to build a large ship—an ark—to save his family and every kind of animal, bird, and creeping thing. God destroyed every living creature on the earth except those inside the ark.

Paul. This apostle is the most influential interpreter of Jesus' message and teaching. Paul was an early Christian missionary who wrote most of the books of the New Testament, which are actually letters to local congregations and individuals. He is the dominant character in Acts, and the person who most vigorously offered the gospel to Gentiles.

Peter or Simon Peter. His Greek name is *Petros,* which means "stone." Jesus changed his name to Peter. This man became the foremost among the twelve disciples. Roman Catholics believe he was the first pope.

Philip. The New Testament lists two Philips.

1. *One of the twelve apostles.*

2. *One of the seven chosen to care for the widows in the church in Jerusalem.* When persecution broke out in Jerusalem, Philip went to Samaria, where he preached and saw many healings.

Rahab. She was a harlot in Jericho who hid two spies sent by Joshua. When Jericho fell to the Israelites, they spared only Rahab and those people inside her house. She later married a man from Judah and became an ancestor of Jesus.

Ruth. A woman of the country of Moab, Ruth was the widowed daughter-in-law of Naomi. She married Boaz and became the great-grandmother of David.

Samson. An Israelite judge noted for his conflicts with the Philistines. He was a man of enormous physical strength but of weak moral character. Delilah learned the secret of his strength and told the Philistines, who cut off his hair and gouged out his eyes. They forced him to grind at the prison mill. Samson's hair—the secret of his strength—grew again. The Philistines sent for the blind Samson so they could laugh at him. He felt for the pillars, on which the house rested, pulled them down, and died with his enemies in the destruction.

Saul.

1. *The Old Testament Saul was the first king of Israel.* He started well, but because of disobedience God rejected him, and David succeeded him.

2. *The other Saul from Tarsus, a persecutor of the church, who was converted on the Damascus road.* His name was changed to Paul, and he became an apostle of Christ and a missionary of the early church. (See *Paul.*)

Shadrach. He was one of the three faithful Hebrews in Babylon who refused to worship the golden image that King Nebuchadnezzar of Babylon set up. For their refusal the three were thrown into a burning furnace, but God preserved all of them.

Solomon. He was the son of King David and Bathsheba and a famous king of Israel. He was noted for his wisdom. The Bible says that because of his marrying many foreign women, his heart was turned from God. Solomon died disillusioned, and the breakup of the monarchy soon followed.

Stephen. One of the seven men chosen by the Jerusalem church to feed Greek-speaking widows. He was a powerful preacher whom the Jews falsely accused and tried for blasphemy. The council stoned Stephen. Acts 7 records his final words, one of the most stirring speeches in the Bible.

Thomas. One of the twelve apostles of Jesus, he is most often remembered for his inability to believe in Jesus' resurrection until he saw and touched Jesus. Through the centuries, he has been called "doubting Thomas." Tradition says he preached in Iran and was martyred in India.

Timothy. Paul found a young Timothy in Lystra, Asia Minor, on his second missionary journey. Timothy followed the apostle on his missionary journeys. Paul referred to Timothy "as a son with his father" (Phil. 2:22). Paul wrote Timothy two letters that are part of the New Testament. They contain fairly strong rebukes as well as words of encouragement.

CHAPTER 25

God's Competitors and Enemies

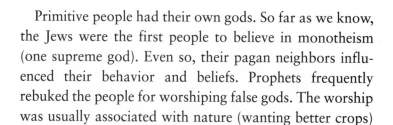

Primitive people had their own gods. So far as we know, the Jews were the first people to believe in monotheism (one supreme god). Even so, their pagan neighbors influenced their behavior and beliefs. Prophets frequently rebuked the people for worshiping false gods. The worship was usually associated with nature (wanting better crops) or fertility (more children and more animals).

Early in the development of Israel's understanding, evil came to be concretized in specific persons or events. Later, it came to be understood as a separate and pervasive power in the created order, as if God had a competitor or antagonist leading the forces of wickedness. This system has a leader called Satan or the Devil, who exercises control over numerous underlings, usually referred to as demons. (See chapter 14.)

The Israelites of Old Testament times came into contact with Canaanites, Egyptians, Babylonians, and other people who worshiped false gods. Repeatedly, God warned the chosen people not to imitate their pagan neighbors, but the

Israelites disobeyed. They slipped into paganism again and again.

How did paganism pull the Israelites away from the true God? To wrestle with the question helps us to understand that ultimately the Jews came to see that God is one and there is no other. By New Testament times, there were no warnings for the Jews to turn from idols. They had learned their lesson in Babylon.

Here are two things to bear in mind. First, we're at least two thousand years away from those pagan cultures. We have only a few texts and artifacts to build on. Consequently, it's difficult to say much about the pagan cultures outside of what the Bible tells us.

Second, we live in a pluralistic society in which we can believe or disbelieve whatever we choose. That wasn't true in ancient times. Agnostics or atheists simply didn't exist— at least that we know of. Such a nonbeliever would have had difficulty living among the Egyptians, Hittites, Greeks, or Romans. Religion was everywhere and at the core of primitive societies. People worshiped the deities of their town, city, or civilization. If they moved to a new location (which was rare) or traveled through a foreign land, they respected the deities there.

There seemed to be the idea that gods had geographic boundaries. When people traveled to new countries, the old gods were no longer effective, so the newcomer would naturally serve the gods of the new location.

The Bible says that God sent Jonah to the wicked city of Nineveh: "But Jonah set out to flee to Tarshish from the presence of the LORD" (Jon. 1:3 NRSV). It is possible that the man believed he could get beyond the sphere of Yahweh's power by going into another area.

Part of the growth of God's people was not only to hear that he was one, but to learn—too often by sad experience—that God was one, the only one, and the great power in all the earth.

Pagan Gods

Religion has always been part of civilization. In the ancient world, it was a powerful force. Pagan civilizations worshiped many gods. The forces of nature that people couldn't control or understand were considered supernatural powers. Thus, they worshiped and feared them. Often their worship was really to appease the anger of the gods or to manipulate them to give good crops and bring about prosperity.

People worshiped their gods with icons or representative idols, which we call idolatry. Most of those idols were shaped in the form of animals or humans, but sometimes they also represented celestial powers such as the sun, moon, stars, or the forces of nature such as the sea or rain. Some pagan gods focused on life forces such as fertility or death. For instance, if a woman couldn't conceive, she prayed and sacrificed to the god or goddess of fertility. Eventually an elaborate system of beliefs in such natural forces as rain or storms developed.

God forbade Israel to make any kind of image or representation (see Exod. 20:3–6). All through the Old Testament, that fact, as much as anything else in the commands of God, set them apart from their neighbors. Even so, the worship of false gods was not only a continuous influence, but also a serious problem.

We can group pagan religions by looking at four countries and the gods they worshiped.

1. *The gods of Mesopotamia (Modern Iraq and Iran)*. The first reference to pagan worship takes place in the time of Abraham, who lived in that area. They were the gods over heaven, air, and earth, and were personified by Anu, Enlil, and Enki or Ea. Another group controlled the heavenly bodies such as the sun, moon, the planet Venus (the evening star). In Ur, the first home of Abraham, they worshiped the moon god.

A significant god of Mesopotamia was Ada, the god of storms. This pagan god's power covered everything from rain for crops to destructive hurricanes.

2. *The gods of Egypt*. The Egyptian gods threatened the Israelites constantly during their years of slavery and even afterward. The Israelites' deliverance was a spiritual victory, but the old ways of thinking from their four hundred years of slavery lingered.

Egyptian religion reflected similar ideas from the ancient world, but they used different figures and names. Their supreme deity was Ra (or Re), the sun god, which was represented as a man with the head of a hawk or falcon, crowned with a solar disk and the figure of the sacred asp.

The great plagues Yahweh sent before the Exodus struck at the heart of Egypt's religion and showed the powerlessness of all these pagan gods. For instance, their fertile land was struck with plagues and the water of the sacred Nile River was turned into blood. Their glorious sun was darkened.

3. *The gods of Canaan.* Canaan was the Promised Land into which the Israelites went. The inhabitants worshiped many gods. Baal was the most prominent, who provided fertility for crops and livestock, and was depicted in many forms and under several different names.

Baal's lover was Anat (or Anath), the goddess of war, love, and fertility. Sometimes Asherah (1 Kings 15:13) was portrayed in Canaan mythology as Baal's wife, and she was also a favorite deity of Egypt.

Others gods were Molech, the national deity of the Ammonites, whose worship was accompanied by the burning of children offered as sacrifices by their own parents. Very similar was Chemosh, the national god of Moab. Ashtoreth was the ancient Syrian and Phoenician goddess of the moon, sexuality, sensual love, and fertility.

Human Enemies of God

The Bible also pictures people who opposed God. Below are many of those mentioned in the Bible. They opposed God either directly or by failing to obey the divine commands.

Achan. This man unintentionally brought about the Israelites' defeat at Ai (Josh. 7:1–24), the nation's second battle and the only defeat they suffered when going into the land. During the destruction of Jericho, Achan had taken some gold, silver, and clothing, and hidden them. Yet before the battle God had forbidden them to do that. Because of his sin, Israel was cursed and defeated in the next battle. God told Joshua to have Achan stoned.

Ahab was an early king of Israel. Under the influence of Jezebel his wife, Ahab gave Baal equal place with God.

He reigned over Israel for twenty-two years (about 873–853 B.C.).

Athaliah. This wicked queen of Judah for six years was the daughter of the evil King Ahab and Queen Jezebel. When her son, King Ahaziah, died, she killed all the heirs except for young Joash, who was hidden in the temple.

Cain. The firstborn son of Adam and Eve. Cain killed his brother Abel, was cursed by God and became a wanderer.

Felix. Emperor Claudius had appointed Felix the governor of Judea. Following a riot in Jerusalem, Paul was taken to Caesarea, where he appeared for a trial before Felix. The governor listened to Paul's defense, eventually adjourned the hearing, and ordered Paul to be kept under open arrest. He allowed the apostle's friends to visit. When Felix was recalled two years later by Nero, Paul was still a prisoner (Acts 24).

Festus. Porcius Festus succeeded Felix as the governor of Judea. He listened to Paul's defense and wanted to send him to stand trial at Jerusalem. But Paul, fearing for his life if he was returned there, appealed to Caesar, and Festus sent him to Rome.

Goliath. A Philistine giant whom David killed with a stone hurled from his slingshot. Scholars estimate that Goliath was about nine feet tall.

Haman. He was the evil, scheming prime minister of Ahasuerus (Xerxes I), king of Persia (485–464 B.C.). When Mordecai, Queen Esther's uncle, refused to bow to him, Haman plotted to destroy Mordecai and all the Jews in the Persian Empire. Esther intervened and saved her people.

Haman was hanged on the very gallows he had constructed for Mordecai.

Herod. Several Roman rulers in the Palestine region shortly before Jesus' ministry and after his resurrection.

1. *Herod the Great (37–4 B.C.)* was the eldest son of Herod Antipater. The title refers not so much to Herod's greatness as to the fact of being the oldest. For thirty-three years he remained a loyal ally of Rome. Later, he was appointed as king of Judea, where he was in direct control of the Jewish people. Jesus was born in Bethlehem during his reign.

2. *Herod Archelaus (4 B.C.–A.D. 6).* He inherited his father's vices without his abilities. He was responsible for much bloodshed in Judea and Samaria. Jewish revolts were brutally crushed.

3. *Herod Philip the Tetrarch (exact dates unknown).* Philip, probably the best of Herod's sons, inherited the northern part of his father Herod the Great's kingdom (Luke 3:1).

4. *Herod Antipas (4 B.C–A.D. 39).* Another of Herod the Great's sons, he began as tetrarch over Galilee and Perea and ruled over Judea during Jesus' life and ministry. Antipas's contacts with Jesus occurred during the period of John the Baptist's ministry. At the trial of Jesus, Antipas couldn't find anything in the charges against Jesus that deserved death, so he sent Jesus back to Pilate.

5. *Herod Agrippa I (A.D. 41–44).* Agrippa took over Antipas's territory after Antipas fell from Rome's favor. Agrippa's power and responsibilities extended far beyond his ability. Apparently, Agrippa wanted to win the favor of his Jewish subjects by opposing the Christians.

6. *Herod Agrippa II (A.D. 50–100)*. Because Emperor Claudius judged Agrippa II too young to assume leadership over all the territory of his father, Agrippa I, he was appointed as the legitimate ruler over only part of this territory. The only reference to Agrippa II in the New Testament occurs in Acts 25:13–26:32, which deals with Paul's imprisonment in Caesarea.

Jezebel. A princess of Tyre and wife of King Ahab of Israel, she worshiped Baal, brought in priests from Tyre, and persecuted the prophets of God. When Jehu came into power, he had Jezebel thrown from a high palace window and she died. Dogs ate her dead body.

Judas Iscariot. One of the twelve disciples, he betrayed Jesus for thirty pieces of silver. After Jesus' condemnation, Judas repented and brought back the money to the priests. They refused to accept it, so he threw down the silver and went out and hanged himself.

Nebuchadnezzar. The emperor of Babylon was the most famous ruler of his day. He defeated Judah, the Southern Kingdom, and made it a vassal state. Because of the continued rebellion of the Jews, he attacked Jerusalem three times, looted the treasury, and carried many of the leading people into exile. In 586/7 B.C., the city fell for the third time and Nebuchadnezzar's army broke down the walls, burned the gates, and destroyed everything.

Pilate, Pontius. He was a Roman governor, of Judea. He sentenced Jesus to be crucified.

Rehoboam. Son and successor of King Solomon, he refused to lighten the tax load of the nation. Ten of the tribes revolted under the leadership of Jeroboam. Only the tribes of Judah and Benjamin (the Southern Kingdom) remained loyal. Rehoboam was a bad king who encouraged pagan customs.

CHAPTER 26

In God's Special Service

Throughout the period of time covered by the Bible, leaders, groups, offices, factions, sects, and organizations arose. Here are some of those who greatly influenced the world in their time. These were men and women who were in God's service. Here is a brief look at their service and position.

Bishop

The Greek word for bishop, *episkopos,* means "overseer." Although the New Testament isn't clear, it probably was similar to the term *elder* or *pastor*—charged with the responsibility of spiritual leadership in a local church in New Testament times.

Before the church was founded, the *episkopos* referred to local gods who watched over people or countries. The word was later applied to people, including those who held positions as magistrates or other government officers. Eventually the term was extended to refer to officials in religious communities with various functions, including those who supervised the revenues of pagan temples. It was a term adopted early as an office in the church.

Deacon

The word meant "servant" or "minister." Today, a deacon is usually a lay officer in many Christian churches. The deacon as a servant of the church is well established in the Bible and church history. But the exact nature of the office is hard to define, because of changing concepts and varying practices among congregations through the centuries.

Judges

These were charismatic military heroes or deliverers who led the nation of Israel against their enemies during the period between the death of Joshua and the establishment of the kingship. The stories of their exploits are found primarily in the Book of Judges.

During the period of the judges, from about 1380 to 1050 B.C., the government of Israel was a loose confederation of tribes gathered about their central shrine, the ark of the covenant. Without a human king to guide them, the people tended to rebel and frequently began to worship false gods. The Book of Judges describes those chaotic times this way: "In those days there was no king in Israel; all the people did what was right in their own eyes" (Judg. 17:6 NRSV). To punish the Israelites, God sent enemy nations to oppress them.

Then the people would repent and cry out to God for help. God would appoint a judge. That person rallied the people and defeated the enemies. The results of the judges' work were often short-lived, and the Israelites would soon enter another stage of rebellion and idolatry, only to see the cycle of oppression and deliverance repeated again.

The judges themselves were a diverse lot. Some of them receive only a brief mention in the Book of Judges. The careers of others, such as Ehud, Jephthah, Gideon, Samson, and Deborah, are explored in greater detail.

Minister

To be a minister was to serve or to be a servant. In the Old Testament, the word was used primarily for court servants (see 1 Kings 10:5; Esth. 1:10). During the period between the Old Testament and the New Testament, the term came to be used in connection with ministering to the poor. That use of the word is close to the work of the seven in waiting on tables in the New Testament (Acts 6:1–7).

Paul urged the pastor-teacher to equip the saints so they could serve one another.

The model, of course, is Jesus, who "did not come to be served, but to serve" (Mark 10:45). Jesus' servanthood radically revised the ethics of Jew and Greek alike because he equated service to God with service to others.

The concept is strengthened by the use of the Greek word *doulos*—the term for "bondslave." This was a person who had been offered freedom but voluntarily turned it down to remain a servant. This idea typified Jesus' purpose to "give his life as a ransom for many" (Mark 10:45).

Apostle

The apostles were special messengers of Jesus Christ, people to whom Jesus delegated authority for certain tasks. The word *apostle* usually refers to the original twelve disciples whom Jesus sent out to preach and heal during his ministry in Galilee, and it's also the first time the word is used (cf. Mark 3:14). The same disciples, with the exception of Judas Iscariot, were recommissioned by Jesus after the resurrection to be his witnesses throughout the world.

The word *apostle* was sometimes used in the New Testament in a wider general sense of "messenger." For instance, when delegates of Christian communities were charged with conveying those churches' contributions to a charitable fund, they were described by Paul as "messengers [apostles] of the churches" (2 Cor. 8:23 NRSV).

In the letters of Paul, he used the word *apostles* to refer to others who, like himself, were not included in the original twelve but who had experienced the risen Christ and were commissioned by him. Paul based his apostleship on the direct call of the exalted Lord, who appeared to him on the Damascus road, and on the Lord's blessing of his ministry in winning converts and establishing churches.

Early in the church's history it was agreed that apostles to the Jews and Gentiles should be divided, with Paul and Barnabas evangelizing the Gentiles. Peter, John, and James (the Lord's brother) were to continue evangelizing Jews.

Paul also counted James, the Lord's brother and not one of the Twelve, an apostle (Gal. 1:19). When Paul said Jesus was seen not only by James but also by "all the apostles" (1 Cor. 15:7), he seems to be describing a wider group than the original twelve.

Evangelist

This word referred to a person authorized to proclaim the gospel of Christ. The word means "one who proclaims good tidings" (see Eph. 4:11; 2 Tim. 4:5).

Apparently, evangelists were not attached to a specific local church but traveled over a wide geographical area, preaching to those to whom the Holy Spirit led them, and especially in reaching out to unbelievers.

Pastor

Pastors were the feeders, protectors, and guides (or shepherds) of flocks of God's people in New Testament times. In speaking of spiritual gifts, Paul wrote that the gifts Christ gave were that "some would be apostles, some prophets, some evangelists, some pastors and teachers" (Eph. 4:11 NRSV). Many believe that pastor-teacher was one office.

Preacher

Preachers proclaimed God's saving message to the people. John the Baptist called for repentance in preparation for the Messiah's appearance; Jesus and the apostles preached in homes, by the seaside, on the temple steps, and in the synagogues. The zeal generated by the coming of the Holy Spirit at Pentecost, coupled with growing persecution of the young church, led the disciples to preach everywhere in the known world.

The distinction between preaching and teaching made in the church today wasn't evident in the New Testament. Both Jesus and Paul regarded themselves as preacher-teachers. For example, Jesus taught the people and preached the gospel (Luke 20:1). Paul testified that he was appointed "a preacher, an apostle, and a teacher" (2 Tim. 1:11 NLT) of the Gentiles.

Prophet

Prophets spoke for God. In the Old Testament, they communicated that message to the nation of Israel; in the New Testament, they became God's "mouthpieces" for the church.

Prophets received their call directly from God. The prophetic call enabled men (and a few women) not to be intimidated or threatened by their audiences. Except for God's call, prophets had no special qualifications. They appeared from all walks of life and classes of society.

Teacher

Teachers instruct or impart knowledge and information. As used in the New Testament, the concept of teaching usually means instruction in the faith. Although some have tried to make a distinction between preaching and teaching, the Bible doesn't support this position. In the list of spiritual offices in Ephesians 4:11, most scholars now see pastor-teacher as a single office.

Priest

Priests were the official ministers or worship leaders in Israel. They represented the people before God and conducted various rituals to atone for their sins. Before the days of the Mosaic Law, the father of a family or the head of a tribe carried out this function. God's appointment of Aaron as the first high priest formally established the priesthood. Aaron's descendants became the priestly line. They carried out the important duties from generation to generation as a special class devoted to God's service.

The Bible often speaks of priests and Levites as if these two offices were the same. They were closely related in that both priests and Levites sprang from a common ancestor—Levi, the son of Jacob. Yet the priests—a specific branch of Levites descended through Aaron—and Levites—all descendants of Levi in general—performed different duties.

Priests officiated at worship by presenting various offerings on behalf of the nation and in leading the people to confess their sins. The Levites assisted the priests. They took care of the tabernacle (later the temple) and performed menial tasks such as providing music, serving as doorkeepers, and preparing sacrifices for offering by the priests.

By the New Testament era, the position of priests had changed considerably. Temple functions were taken over by the "chief priests" while scribes and Pharisees—two special groups that arose to present the law and interpret its meaning for the people, overshadowed ordinary priests. In spite of their diminished role, Jesus respected the office of priest and called on the priests to witness his healing of lepers in keeping with the law.

The priests were some of the most zealous opponents of Jesus. As leaders of the Sanhedrin (the Jewish high court), they bore much of the responsibility for his crucifixion. They also led the opposition to the apostles and the early church.

CHAPTER 27

This We Believe

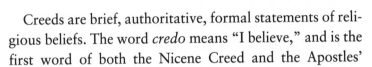

Creeds are brief, authoritative, formal statements of religious beliefs. The word *credo* means "I believe," and is the first word of both the Nicene Creed and the Apostles' Creed.

The first creed of the early church was simply, "Jesus is Lord." As the church spread across the world, the need arose to formalize what the orthodox (true) church believed. Most of the time, they were also positive statements against heretical teachings.

To form the first significant creed—called the Nicene Creed—church leaders met and formulated a statement about God, Jesus, and the Holy Spirit. The creed states only what the church officially believed. This creed rallied against Arius. (See chapter 7.)

In time, formalized creeds emerged, usually recited at baptisms and worship services. The two earliest and most historically significant of the church are the Nicene Creed and the Apostles' Creed.

The Nicene Creed

This creed was adopted by the Council of Nicaea in A.D.
325 and revised by the Council of Constantinople in 381.
The Council of Nicaea, convened by the Roman emperor
Constantine the Great (ruled 306–337), rejected a heresy
known as Arianism, which denied the divinity of Jesus.
The Nicene Creed formally proclaimed the divinity and
equality of Jesus Christ, the Son of God, in the Trinity. It
reads as follows:

I believe in one God the Father Almighty, Maker
of heaven and earth, and of all things visible and
invisible; And in one Lord Jesus Christ, the only-
begotten Son of God, begotten of His Father before
all worlds; God of God; Light of Light; Very God
of Very God; Begotten, not made; Being of one
substance with the Father, by whom all things were
made; Who for us men, and for our salvation,
came down from heaven; And was incarnate by the
Holy Ghost of the Virgin Mary, and was made
man; And was crucified also for us under Pontius
Pilate. He suffered and was buried; And the third
day He rose again according to the Scriptures; And
ascended into heaven; And sitteth on the right
hand of the Father. And He shall come again with
glory to judge both the quick and the dead; Whose
kingdom shall have no end.

And I believe in the Holy Ghost; The Lord and
Giver of Life; Who proceedeth from the Father and
the Son; Who with the Father and the Son together
is worshipped and glorified; Who spake by the
prophets. And I believe one Holy Catholic and

Apostolic Church. I acknowledge one Baptism for the remission of sins. And I look for the Resurrection of the dead; And the Life of the world to come. Amen.

The Apostles' Creed

This well-known creed creates the basis of most other religious statements of belief. Although it bears the name of the apostles, it did not originate with them, or at least not all of it. Not until the sixth century did the Apostles' Creed appear in its present form. Even so, this creed has held an important place through the centuries and is still recited in many churches around the world in each worship service. It reads as follows:

I believe in God the Father Almighty, Maker of heaven and earth; And in Jesus Christ His only Son our Lord; who was conceived by the Holy Ghost, born of the Virgin Mary, suffered under Pontius Pilate, was crucified, dead, and buried; He descended into hell; the third day He rose again from the dead; He ascended into heaven, and sitteth on the right hand of God the Father Almighty; from thence He shall come to judge the quick and the dead.

I believe in the Holy Ghost; the holy Catholic Church; the communion of saints; the forgiveness of sins; the resurrection of the body; and the life everlasting. Amen.

CHAPTER 28

All Those Miracles

We tend to downplay a lot of the more-than-natural events of the Bible. Maybe it's because we don't see those obvious acts of God that fill the biblical pages. Some people discount miracles as observations by the ignorant. They just didn't understand certain natural laws.

"People weren't raised from the dead," someone once said to me. "They were in comas."

He had no answer when I asked, "Then why did those people snap out of the coma at that moment? Why not the day before or a week later?"

I can't explain most miracles. Because I believe the Bible is God's infallible Word to the world, I accept miracles—even if I don't understand many of them.

In the Bible God speaks, acts, and performs miracles. These events show the heavenly power at work. Why not? This is the only God, the God who controls the universe. This is the God who cares, and the caring shows itself sometimes by speeding up or overriding natural laws.

Miracles are recorded in the Bible—but not everywhere within the sacred pages. They're largely confined to three distinct periods. Other more-than-natural happenings occur, but they're usually isolated events, such as during the period of the judges. Two outstanding miracles occur in the Book of Daniel. They are the saving of the three young men thrown into the hot furnace and Daniel's deliverance from a den of lions.

I'm focusing on those three significant periods of miracles in the Bible.

From Moses to the Promised Land

This includes the miracles before the people left Egypt and during their forty years of wandering in the wilderness.

The miracles include the ten plagues that showed God's sovereign power in judgment and salvation. In dividing the waters of the Red Sea, God showed loving protection for Israel as well as judgment on Egypt for its failure to recognize God. The Amalekites were defeated in battle because Aaron and Hur held Moses' hands high, apparently for hours, until Joshua and his troops won.

A variety of miracles happened during the wilderness journey. One of the earliest and most long-lasting was the provision of manna each morning (see Exod. 16:1–36). This mysterious food became the primary diet of at least a million people for forty years.

This period shows the great lengths to which God went to provide for every need of the chosen people. Some miracles were done to convince unbelievers such as Pharaoh, others to show that God had chosen Moses to lead and not Miriam or a band of renegade priests. Many miracles were acts of love, such as sending quail to feed the people or turning bitter water into what they could drink.

A few miracles occurred after they entered the land, such as crossing the Jordan River on dry land and the fall of the walls of Jericho. In another battle, the sun "stood still" until Joshua and his armies had won the victory. But after the Israelites enter the land, miracles become rare.

The Period of Elijah and Elisha

In 1 and 2 Kings are recorded approximately twenty-five miracles performed by these two prophets. These occurred at a low period in the life of Israel. The two prophets lived in the part of Israel where the ten tribes had broken away and formed their own kingdom.

The most memorable miracle of the period was when Elijah prayed and it didn't rain for three years. When he prayed again, the rains poured within hours. He successfully challenged the pagan priests of Baal on Mount Carmel.

Elijah's protégé, Elisha, became the leading voice for God. The Bible describes about twice as many miracles by the hand of Elisha as it does by his mentor. After Elisha's death, the miracles stopped.

The Ministry of Jesus
Through the Acts of the Apostles

The period covered by the New Testament is the third great period of miracles in the Bible. The miracles started when Jesus began his public ministry. From then on, everywhere he went, Jesus taught about God, but he also healed and performed miracles.

Why did Jesus perform miracles? When he was in prison, John the Baptist sent some of his disciples to ask Jesus if he was the promised Messiah. Instead of answering the question, Jesus told them to report to John what they saw and heard: "The blind receive sight, the lame walk, those who have leprosy are cured, the deaf hear, the dead are raised, and the good news is preached to the poor" (Matt. 11:4–5). He pointed to miracles as the fulfillment of the promises of the Messiah as foretold in places such as Isaiah 35:5–6; 61:1.

Jesus also raised the dead, provided food for more than five thousand people with nothing but a boy's lunch, and stopped a raging storm on Lake Gennesseret.

Jesus started it; the apostles and early Christians kept the pace going. Acts is a book of miracles, because the supernatural events continued, especially through Peter and Paul. In fact, after the coming of the Holy Spirit in chapter 2, it's difficult to read far without something supernatural taking place.

This is undoubtedly the great period of healings. For example, God "did extraordinary miracles through Paul, so that even handkerchiefs and aprons that had touched him were taken to the sick, and their illnesses were cured and the evil spirits left them" (Acts 19:11–12).

Spiritual Gifts

Not only is the New Testament a time of miracles, there are portions that speak about spiritual gifts or supernatural talents by God's people, and they're not limited to one or two prophets. Both Paul and Peter refer to such gifts, which were apparently an accepted element of the early church.

The lists of the gifts of the Spirit in the New Testament show that using signs and wonders—miracles—were ways by which believers ministered to others inside and outside the church (Rom. 12:6–8; 1 Cor 12:8–10, 28–30; Eph. 4:11–12).

Different lists of spiritual gifts appear: 1 Corinthians 12, 14; Romans 12:3–8; Ephesians 4:7–12; and 1 Peter 4:10–11. They're not written as all-inclusive lists. In each case, they speak of certain aspects of ministry in the early church.

Paul makes it clear that all gifts were equally valid, but not equally valuable. Their value was determined by the need in the church. In explaining to the Corinthians— endowed with gifts but engaged in much strife among themselves—Paul used the analogy of the human body. All members of the body, he said, have functions, but some are more important than others.

He tied in the Trinity by saying that there are different gifts but all come from the same Spirit; different forms of service, but the same Lord for all, and a variety of working, "but the same God works all of them" in everyone (1 Cor. 12:6).

The most prominent passage about gifts comes from 1 Corinthians 12:8–10. Here are the nine gifts Paul mentions.

1. *The message of wisdom.* This probably refers to guidance, such as the time church leaders worshiped and fasted. "The Holy Spirit said, 'Set apart for me Barnabas

and Saul for the work to which I have called them'"
(Acts 13:2).

2. *Message of knowledge.* This meant specific knowledge that couldn't be figured out from study or observation. Acts 5:1–9 is one example, where Peter spoke of the
behavior of a couple about things he had no way of
knowing.

3. *Faith.* Obviously more than the ability to believe
God, most likely this referred to extraordinary faith—the
ability to believe for miracles or great events.

4. *Healings.* Because the word is plural, possibly those
who had this gift were able to heal only limited types of
diseases.

5. *Miracles.* These are the events that defy natural explanation. For example, an angry crowd at Lystra stoned Paul
and left him for dead. "But after the disciples had gathered
around him, he got up and went back into the city" (Acts
14:20).

6. *Prophecy.* Although this can be, as in other places,
speaking the mind of God, in the New Testament, it seems
primarily a gift to speak of the future, such as when
Agabus the prophet foretold a great famine that would
come upon Israel.

7. *The ability to distinguish between spirits.* This was
probably the ability to detect or discern the false from the
real.

8. *Speaking in tongues or other languages.* Speaking in
tongues was a prominent gift mentioned several times. Its
value was that messages were given in languages unknown
to the speaker (as on the day of Pentecost), but the native
listeners could understand.

9. *Interpretation of tongues.* Paul stated that unless an interpreter was present in worship services, speaking in tongues had no value.

CHAPTER 29

Jewish Religious Factions

By the time of Jesus, Judaism had become a sectarian religion. Jews differed on what they believed. They had long left the writings of the Hebrew Scriptures as their only source of guidance. They had divided and spent many hours debating questions on just about every topic. Here are three of their favorites:

- Who is a true Jew?
- What does God require of Israel?
- What is the destiny of Israel?

Their conflicting answers revealed sharp differences between the sects of the time. When Jesus was born, there were three dominant sects: Pharisees, Sadducees, and Essenes. Many splinter groups also existed. Within each of these divisions, small groups rallied around the teachings of a particular rabbi or his school of thought.

The Major Factions

Pharisees. The name probably means "pure ones." They were the master interpreters of the oral traditions of the rabbis. Most of them came from middle-class families of artisans and tradesmen (for example, Paul was a tent-maker). They exerted a powerful influence over the peasant masses.

The historian Josephus observed that when the Jewish people faced an important decision, they relied on the opinion of the Pharisees rather than that of the king or high priest. Because the people trusted them, the Pharisees moved into many high government positions, including the Sanhedrin.

Pharisees believed in the resurrection—that righteous people would live again after death and the wicked would be punished for eternity. Not many other Jewish groups accepted this view. Instead, the others held to the Greek and Persian idea that death permanently separated the soul from the body.

Sadducees. This sect was the guardian of the Torah (or Law). After the Maccabees drove out the Syrians, a group that became known as the Sadducees endorsed Greek ideas and applied Greek logic to the problems of the day.

We're not sure what their name meant. There are two possibilities. It may come from the Hebrew word *saddig,* meaning "righteous." Or, because they were connected with the temple priesthood, the name may come from the priestly name of Zadok.

The Sadducees rejected the oral tradition of the rabbis and accepted only the written Law of Moses—what we call the first five books of the Bible—and condemned any teaching not based on the written words of those books. The Sadducees adopted the beliefs of the Greek philosopher Epicurus, who held that the soul dies with the body.

They objected to the Persian influences in the teachings of the Pharisees, such as their acceptance of angels, demons, and resurrection. Thus, they opposed Jesus when he agreed with the Pharisees.

Paul, in making his defense of the faith before the Sanhedrin, caused an uproar by bringing up issues such as angels and the resurrection. The two groups became so enraged that the Roman commander feared they would kill Paul, so he rescued him (Acts 23).

Essenes. The Essenes were the righteous radicals, but they aren't named in the Bible, although some believe John the Baptist was one of them. This sect emerged from the pious movement known as the Hasideans—the followers of the Maccabbees.

The word *Essene* comes from a Hebrew word that means "pious" or "holy." Although other Jews called them by this name, Essenes themselves probably rejected the label. Historical evidence suggests they didn't consider themselves to be especially pious. They did see themselves as the guardians of a body of mysterious truths that would govern the life of Israel after the Messiah appeared. The Essenes planned to keep this information secret until the proper time.

The Essenes practiced elaborate rites to purify themselves physically and spiritually. By avoiding the corruption of the society around them, they believed God would honor their faithfulness.

Most of the Essenes lived communally in remote desert areas. We have gotten this information from the Dead Sea Scrolls. The scrolls don't identify the people who lived in the Qumran community where the scrolls were written, but the Roman historian Pliny said that area was their headquarters.

In 1947, a Bedouin shepherd boy cast a stone into a cave at Khirbet Qumran, near the Dead Sea, and heard the breaking of a clay jar. The boy entered the cave and found several jars containing ancient manuscripts. Scholars identified them as the Book of Isaiah, a commentary on Habakkuk, and several documents that contained the teachings of the Qumran sect.

Eventually, they located eleven caves that contained ancient scrolls and fragments. The caves yielded fragments or copies of every book of the Old Testament except Esther. Most of the manuscripts had been written in the time of the Maccabees. This discovery sparked archaeologists' interest in the ruins of Khirbet Qumran itself, where they found a large room for copying manuscripts.

Scholars still debate whether the people of Qumran were actually Essenes, since their writings disagree with known Essene teachings at several points. If the people of Qumran were simply another splintered Essene group, that would account for their occasional departures from the mainstream of Essene teachings.

Zealots. Pompey's invasion of Palestine in 63 B.C. destroyed the Jews' hopes of restoring their own government. Yet the Zealots stubbornly insisted that the Jews must repel the Roman invaders, and they tried to stir up rebellion among the Jews.

The best-known Zealot leader was Judas, the Galilean who led an ill-fated revolt against the Romans. This was the beginning of the Jews' conflicts with the Roman

Empire, which ended with the destruction of the temple in
A.D. 70.

During Felix's term as procurator of Judea (A.D 52–60),
the Zealots formed a radical group known as the Sicarii
("dagger people") and circulated in crowds during festi-
vals. They killed Roman sympathizers with daggers they
concealed in their clothing.

During the war with Rome (A.D. 66–70), the Sicarii
escaped to the old Jewish fortress at Masada and made it
their headquarters. Two years after the fall of Jerusalem, a
Roman legion laid siege to Masada. Rather than die at the
hands of the Gentiles, the Sicarii killed themselves and
their families—960 people in all.

Herodians. Another Jewish sect known as the
Herodians emerged during the Roman era. A political
rather than a religious group, they were able to include
those with varying religious viewpoints. They supported
the dynasty of Herod the Great. They seemed to prefer
Herod's oppressive home rule to Rome's foreign supervi-
sion. The Herodians are mentioned three times in the New
Testament, but none of the references give us a clear picture of their beliefs.

Samaritans. The Samaritans were descendants of the
Jews who remained in Palestine after the Assyrians
defeated Israel in the eighth century B.C. They came from
mixed marriages between Jews and Assyrian settlers who
entered the Promised Land.

The Samaritans worshiped God on Mount Gerizim,
where they built their own temple and sacrificed animals.
The Jews who returned from the Babylonian Exile
despised the Samaritans. In 128 B.C. John Hyrcanus

destroyed the temple on Mount Gerizim. From that point on, Jews and Samaritans had no dealings with each other.

Jesus' Response to the Factions

By the first century, the sects of Israel had changed the character of the Jewish faith. The straight course that God originally had set before Israel had become a winding path through mysticism, Greek humanism, and ritualistic traditions.

Jesus often responded to the misguided ideas of those groups and confronted their traditional sources of authority with a truer understanding of the law. Not only did Jesus denounce the scribes and Pharisees for their hypocrisy and self-righteousness, but he especially chided the Pharisees for their superficial methods of observing the Sabbath.

The New Testament never shows Jesus speaking directly to the Essenes, but it's likely that their peculiar system of authority had displaced the authority of God and the coming Messiah, as the other Jewish sects had done.

CHAPTER 30

What Are the Words of God?
The Old Testament

What are the words of God? That's easy. They're the words found in the Bible. And, as I point out in the next chapter, they are the *inspired* words.

The Bible consists of sixty-six books, written over a period of about sixteen hundred years. This and the following chapter survey those books and point out their essential message.

Our word *Bible* comes from the Greek word that means "books." The Jewish sacred writings have twenty-four books, but they contain the same material as the thirty-nine books in the Christian version of the Old Testament.

How can that be? It happened like this. Jewish scholars organized the Old Testament into three major sections: the Law (the five books of Moses, or Torah), the Prophets, and the Writings. The books were then arranged according to the official status of the writers—Moses, the prophets, and the other writers. The sequence had nothing

229

to do with inspiration, because they believed that all the books of their Bible are equally inspired and authoritative.

Order of the Hebrew Old Testament

The order of the twenty-four books in the Hebrew Bible is as follows:

The Law. Genesis, Exodus, Leviticus, Numbers, and Deuteronomy.

The Prophets.

The former prophets. Joshua, Judges, 1 and 2 Samuel, 1 and 2 Kings (what we call the books of Samuel and Kings were one book).

The latter prophets. Isaiah, Jeremiah, Ezekiel, and the Twelve, which was one book (Hosea, Joel, Amos, Obadiah, Jonah, Micah, Nahum, Habbakuk, Zephaniah, Haggai, Zechariah, and Malachi).

The Writings. Psalms, Proverbs, Job, Song of Solomon, Ruth, Lamentations, Ecclesiastes, Esther, Daniel, Ezra, Nehemiah, 1 and 2 Chronicles (as one book).

Then came the difference, brought about by Jerome, who translated the Old Testament into Latin in the fourth century A.D. Jerome's order of the books in the Vulgate was based on the topics rather than the importance of the writers. He also divided them into thirty-nine books.

Christians today follow Jerome's order. He also included books called deuterocanonical or apocryphal. Other than Roman Catholics, Christian denominations don't consider them part of the Bible, so I haven't listed them.

Five Groups of Old Testament Books

We usually divide the thirty-nine books of the Old Testament into five groups. Here are those and a brief overview of their contents.

1. *The books of Moses.* Traditionally, we view the first five books together. Rabbis recognized their close connection and referred to them as "the five-fifths of the law."

The first eleven chapters of Genesis constitute a history of creation and of the early generations of the world. Chapters 12–50 focus on Abraham and his descendants and end with the death of Joseph. The rest of the five books of the law give the history of the Israelites from the death of Joseph to the entrance into Canaan, together with the elaborate code of moral laws and the form of civil government that God revealed to Moses.

2. *The historical books.* These are the twelve books from Joshua to Esther. The historical books provide the history from the death of Moses, the conquest of the land, the establishment of a monarchy, the nation torn into two kingdoms, the destruction of both kingdoms, the Exile in Babylon, and end with the rebuilding of the temple under Nehemiah.

3. *The poetic books.* We give the name of poetry to compositions that possess imaginative thought, figurative language, and an arrangement in lines of regulated lengths and accents. Hebrew poetry has all of this, yet it uses techniques that are quite different from what we find in English-language poems.

4. *The major prophets.* Isaiah, Jeremiah (along with Lamentations), Ezekiel, and Daniel—these writings were

considered more important than the others. They are also longer and cover larger time periods.

5. *The minor prophets.* These are the lesser prophets because they're shorter books and cover a more limited range of topics. They are Hosea, Joel, Amos, Obadiah, Jonah, Micah, Nahum, Habbakuk, Zephaniah, Haggai, Zechariah, and Malachi.

An Overview of the Books of the Old Testament

1. *Genesis.* The first book sets the stage for the rest of the Bible. It surveys God's work of creation and the establishment of a covenant with Abraham's family through Isaac and Jacob. The book ends after Joseph brings his father Jacob and the rest of the clan into Egypt as favored guests of Pharaoh.

2. *Exodus.* Exodus takes up where Genesis leaves off. The period between Joseph and Moses is covered by two verses. The once-favored guests of Pharaoh had become a nation of slaves. After more than four hundred years in the land, God calls Moses to lead the people into the land promised to Abraham. They leave Egypt and move toward the new land. God gives the law and prepares the Israelites to enter Canaan.

3. *Leviticus.* This book continues the narrative of Exodus. It describes the priestly practices and the ritual of worship in ancient Israel.

4. *Numbers.* God teaches the Israelites how to function as a community. They receive laws about such things as worship, civil relationships, and diet and health before they enter Canaan.

5. *Deuteronomy.* This book is quoted about eighty times in the New Testament, more than any other Old Testament book. The title means "second law." It repeats the Ten Commandments. The book contains three messages of instruction and exhortation from Moses, the covenant is renewed, and they are ready to enter the Promised Land.

6. *Joshua.* The Book of Joshua is a book of conquest. Under Joshua's leadership, the Israelites subdue their enemies and settle down in the land God gave them to inherit. The people remain faithful to God during the lifetime of their leader.

7. *Judges.* Judges continues the narrative after Joshua's death. Instead of remaining faithful, the people turn to pagan gods, become enslaved, cry to God for help, and God raises up a judge—a heroic figure who delivers them. They have peace and then the cycle starts again.

8. *Ruth.* In telling the experiences of Ruth, this book gives us a detailed account of Israelite village life in the time of the judges. The book also demonstrates the ancient law of levirate marriage, by which a male relative would marry a dead man's widow to provide offspring to carry the family name. Ruth is important because she was an ancestor of David and, hence, of Jesus.

9. *First Samuel.* This book continues the history of Israel from the period of the judges down to the establishment of the monarchy under Saul. Samuel, who was a priest, is usually regarded as the last judge. The people insist on having a king, and God gives them Saul. The king starts well and ends badly. God then tells Samuel to anoint

David as the next king. For years, David flees from the king. In a final battle, Saul dies.

10. *Second Samuel.* David ascends the throne as the second king. The book describes David's reign objectively, showing both his strengths and weaknesses. He is the most-loved king of all Israel, and through him ran the line of the Messiah.

11. *First Kings.* David's son, Solomon, becomes the nation's third king, and he's known for his vast wisdom. He builds the first temple in Jerusalem. Solomon marries many foreign wives—often to create an alliance with those nations—and those wives lead him astray.

When Solomon dies, his son Rehoboam becomes king. He's harsh and foolish and unwilling to make concessions, so ten of the twelve tribes rebel and form the Northern Kingdom. Israel now has two kingdoms. The books of Kings don't give a detailed history of all the kings of Judah and Israel. They give only passing reference to powerful kings like Omri and Jeroboam II but emphasize the ministry of the prophets Elijah and Elisha. The writer evaluates each king by his obedience or lack of obedience to God.

12. *Second Kings.* Continuing the story, this book describes the fall of the Northern Kingdom to Assyria. It also follows the story through to the last days of Judah, the Southern Kingdom.

13. *First Chronicles.* This book begins by listing the genealogies of many Jewish families. Those records were the only proof of individual rights to priestly office and claims to the property of ancestors. Most of the book centers on David's reign. Kings has a more objective view

whereas Chronicles takes a more spiritual approach to the same events.

14. *Second Chronicles*. This book continues the material from First Chronicles and describes the history of some of the kings in more detail than the books of Kings. For example, it devotes thirty verses to the religious reforms and military exploits of King Asa, although Kings gives us less than half of that material.

15. *Ezra*. The prophet-priest writes about the Jews' return from exile. He leads the reforms and the restoration of worship in Jerusalem.

16. *Nehemiah*. A cupbearer under the Persian monarch, Nehemiah receives permission from the king to go back to Jerusalem and repair the walls surrounding the city. He and Ezra are the two heroes of the time of return and restoration.

17. *Esther*. Jews have valued this book highly as a patriotic rallying point. They like its story of Esther's revenge against the wicked court official Haman, who tries to exterminate the Jews. This is the only book in the Bible that doesn't mention the name of God. That fact troubled Jewish scholars for centuries, but the book has earned its place in the canon by tradition, and it's a telling portrayal of God's hidden hand in providence.

18. *Job*. Written mostly in poetic form, Job tells how God gives Satan freedom to test Job's faith and faithfulness. The man endures the loss of family, money, health, and the respect of his friends. The book addresses the age-old question, "Why do the righteous suffer?"

19. *Psalms*. Often called the songbook of ancient Israel, Psalms contains hymns that the priests sang during temple

worship and ballads that express the feelings of the Hebrew people at different stages in their history. The 150 psalms cover a wide range of emotions. Some of them are personal expressions of faith, doubt, anger, and praise.

20. *Proverbs.* This is a collection of ethical precepts about practical living. Like Psalms, it arranges its material in balanced pairs of thoughts by the method of contrasting parallelism.

21. *Ecclesiastes.* Ecclesiastes blasts the emptiness of greed and materialism and exhorts the reader to "remember your Creator" (Eccl. 12:1).

22. *Song of Solomon.* Probably no book of the Bible has been interpreted in as many different ways as this one. The interpretations fall into two categories—literal and allegorical. The Jewish Talmud teaches that the book is an allegory of God's love for Israel. Many Christians see it as an allegory of God's love for the church.

On the literal side, Theodore of Mopsuestia (fourth century A.D.) believed the book was a straightforward poem that Solomon wrote in honor of his marriage. Others have said the book expresses God's approval of marriage. Some suppose that it's a poetic marriage drama used in ancient times. One viewpoint is that it's an ancient love story with a strong religious and spiritual message. Despite these differing opinions, the book is one of the most beautiful examples of Hebrew poetry in the Old Testament.

23. *Isaiah.* The most famous of the writing prophets proclaimed God's word under a succession of kings, always warning them that God would destroy Judah because of their evil ways. They didn't listen. Tradition

says that King Manasseh executed Isaiah by having him sawed in two.

24. *Jeremiah*. These messages were directed toward the Southern Kingdom just before the nation fell to the Babylonians. Jeremiah is the great prophet and central figure of the book who delivers hard-to-accept messages, experiencing rejection and torture.

25. *Lamentations*. The book consists of five separate elegies or lamentations. The whole book is more elaborately poetical than any other portion of the Bible. In Hebrew, which doesn't show up in English translations, each of the five chapters is arranged in twenty-two portions, corresponding with the twenty-two letters of the Hebrew alphabet.

26. *Ezekiel*. When Nebuchadnezzar captured Jerusalem, he stunned the Israelites. They believed God would never allow their enemies to violate the holy sanctuary. Ezekiel, a captive in Babylon, receives a series of visions from God and writes in vivid, symbolic language. He encourages the people, and the later chapters look forward to restoration from exile and spiritual renewal.

27. *Daniel*. The book is like two books. The first part of the book (chapters 1–6) tells about Daniel's life in the Babylonian court and of various occurrences during the reigns of Nebuchadnezzar, Belshazzar, and Darius. The second half of the book (chapters 7–12) is prophetic and highly symbolic, evoking a wide variety of interpretations. A popular interpretation says the final six chapters predict various political changes, the coming of the Messiah, the rebuilding of Jerusalem and the temple, a subsequent

second destruction of Jerusalem, and the Messiah's return in judgment.

28. *Hosea.* The book consists of threats and denunciations against the wickedness of the Israelites, mingled with predictions of the final restoration of God's people.

29. *Joel.* This short, prophetic book predicts the outpouring of the Spirit of God—a prophecy fulfilled in Acts 2.

30. *Amos.* This prophet writes about Israel neglecting the worship of God and indulging in extravagant luxury. Rich merchants oppress the poor and worship the pagan idols that Jeroboam I had introduced to the nation.

31. *Obadiah.* Obadiah directs his attention to the Edomites and condemns them for joining the other enemies to plunder and burn Jerusalem. He warns that God will judge the Edomites for their actions.

32. *Jonah.* God sends Jonah on a mission to the wicked city of Nineveh to foretell their doom. They repent and God withholds destruction. This book teaches the universal love of God—that Yahweh will forgive the wicked if they repent.

33. *Micah.* The prophet declares God's anger against both Israel and Judah. He delivers his prophecies at different times, and it is difficult to follow the historical sequence of the book.

34. *Nahum.* Nahum is a single poem of great eloquence. Its theme is "The Burden of Nineveh"—the coming punishment of that city and empire in retribution for the Assyrians' cruel treatment of the Jews.

35. *Habakkuk.* Most of this book is a stern warning for the people of Judah. It begins with the startling fact that

God was going to use the sinful Chaldeans (Babylonians) to overpower the Jews. The book closes with a beautiful hymn of petition and praise that the Jews might have sung in their services.

36. *Zephaniah.* Zephaniah lashes out at the people's hypocrisy and idolatrous worship. Even though King Josiah tried to bring reform, they didn't change. Zephaniah foretells that this behavior will lead them to destruction, although there will be a restoration afterward.

37. *Haggai.* The Jews who return from Babylon begin to rebuild the temple. Because their neighbors harassed and discouraged them, they had suspended work on the project. Haggai prods them to finish the task.

38. *Zechariah.* Zechariah not only exhorts the people to rebuild the temple; he also holds out hope for the restored nation.

39. *Malachi.* This short prophetic book was written to rebuke the people for their shallow worship practices. Unlike any other biblical book, portions are written in the form of debate. God makes a statement, the people deny it, and then God refutes their arguments in detail.

CHAPTER 31

What Are the Words of God?
The New Testament

Christians have regarded their collection of Scriptures as being "the Book" since the Council of Carthage drew up the final list of New Testament books in A.D. 397.

The order of the books was based on subject categories: historical books (the Gospels and Acts); letters (beginning with the Pauline collection); and the Apocalypse or Revelation. Early church tradition placed the Gospels in the order they appear today. Those same leaders also arranged the letters of Paul into two categories: *(1) Letters to specific congregations or Christians in geographic areas.* They were generally arranged according to the length of the letters. *(2) Letters to individuals.* These are shorter and less theologically significant.

General letters (or non-Pauline writings) then followed. They placed Hebrews first. Tradition said Paul wrote Hebrews, but the authorship (not the contents) has been in dispute from earliest times. The other letters to James,

Peter, John, and Jude follow, and the Bible closes with Revelation.

This order has remained constant since about the fourth century A.D., but many lists circulating during the first three centuries didn't include all of the books.

Three Groups of New Testament Books

Here are the divisions of the New Testament books and a brief overview of their contents.

1. *The historical books.* The historical books of the New Testament comprise the four Gospels and the Acts of the Apostles. The word *gospel* comes from the Anglo-Saxon words *god* ("good") and *spel* ("word" or "tidings"). Gospel is a literal translation of the Greek *evangelion*, which was probably the title the authors gave to these books.

Bible students often call the first three Gospels *synoptics*, which comes from a Greek word that means "having a single view" or "to see together." In spite of their individual emphases, they give a consecutive account of Jesus' life and actions. John focuses more on themes and the role of Jesus.

The Book of Acts advances the story about thirty years beyond the crucifixion of Jesus. Except for what Acts tells us and incidental statements in the letters, we have to depend on later church and secular history for knowledge of the progress of Christianity.

2. *The letters.* A collection of letters on theology and practical religion forms the second great division of the New Testament. These twenty-one letters were written by five of the apostles—Paul, James, Peter, John, and Jude.

Paul wrote thirteen (fourteen for those who credit him with Hebrews). The apostles wrote these letters to groups of Christian converts or to individuals on different occasions. They were usually the result of problems that had emerged, and the letters are extended answers to their questions.

The letters aren't placed in the order in which they were written, but according to the length of the books and importance of the audiences addressed. Romans comes first because Rome was the capital of the empire. The two Corinthian letters come next because Corinth was an important city in Greece.

Paul's letters to individuals follow those to collective audiences. The first two are to Timothy because of his closeness to Paul, followed by the letter to Titus, and finally Philemon. (Because of uncertainty over authorship, Hebrews appears last and often is listed as one of the general letters.)

After Paul's letters come the seven general letters—so called because they were addressed to Christians generally. They appear roughly in the order of their length.

3. *Apocalyptic.* Revelation, the last book of the New Testament, is a book of visions and symbolism. Bible scholars have interpreted it in many different ways, and it remains the most controversial book of the Bible.

An Overview of the Twenty-seven Books of the New Testament

1. *Matthew.* The apostle Matthew wrote this account of Jesus' life to convince the Jews that Jesus was their Messiah.

2. *Mark*. This may have been the first written Gospel and was directed at Gentile Christians. We can tell that because of the careful way Mark explains religious terms that would have been familiar to the Jews but not to Gentiles.

3. *Luke*. The physician and companion to Paul pointed to Jesus' ministry as the Savior. He said he got his material from other sources and put them together. He likely may have aimed at a Greek-speaking audience. (His Greek is the most educated in the New Testament.)

4. *John*. The material in this Gospel suggests that, while preparing a history of Jesus' life that would supplement the three previous Gospels, John wanted to present the teachings of Jesus Christ in a way that would refute heretical doctrines that were then prevailing among Christians.

5. *Acts of the Apostles*. Acts did two crucial things: It described the Holy Spirit's work in the lives of the early church, and it showed how God brought the Gentiles into the church and broke down the barriers between the two races.

6. *Romans*. In this letter, Paul's most brilliantly reasoned book, he addressed Jewish and Gentile converts. He set forth a body of Christian doctrine so broadly conceived and so fully stated that it would accomplish all Paul could do if he were able to preach in Rome.

7. *First Corinthians*. When most people reflect on this letter, they think of Paul's great rhapsody on Christian love in the thirteenth chapter. The entire book contains a wealth of practical advice on Christian conduct, designed to help the Corinthians deal with the problems in their congregation.

8. *Second Corinthians.* In this letter Paul vindicates his apostleship. He writes of physical weaknesses and persecution from legalizers and, in so doing, discloses his heart more than in any other letter.

9. *Galatians.* This letter refutes the teachings of the Judaizers, who wanted new Christians to be circumcised and to adopt other Jewish rituals. It's a strong letter emphasizing that salvation comes from God without being earned.

10. *Ephesians.* Paul emphasizes that Christ is the head of the church. The core of the letter revolves around Jews and Gentiles being united into one body. He exhorts his fellow Christians to live lives worthy of their high calling as Jesus' disciples.

11. *Philippians.* Paul expresses his thanks to the Philippians for a gift they had sent him in prison. In the process, he warns them to correct some problems arising in the church.

12. *Colossians.* Church leaders said that Gentiles had to adopt Jewish rituals when they became Christians. Those same leaders were apparently dabbling in anti-Christian philosophy, called Gnosticism. Paul attempted to correct such trends.

13. *First Thessalonians.* Paul reminisces about his earlier work in Thessalonica and encourages the Thessalonians to live holy lives. He also explains the destiny of the dead, giving us one of the most detailed discussions of the Christian hope in the New Testament.

14. *Second Thessalonians.* Troublesome times will come before Christ returns. Paul urges believers to guard against

laziness or foolish confidence, and instructs them to make the best use of the time that remains.

15. *First Timothy.* God had given Timothy a trusted ministry. Paul rebukes Timothy and advises the young pastor about proper conduct in dealing with church problems.

16. *Second Timothy.* This letter follows much the same pattern as the first. Here Paul emphasizes the need to pass the gospel on to faithful Christians who would proclaim the good news to succeeding generations.

17. *Titus.* Sound doctrine should produce a godly life. So a minister like Titus needed to do more than teach the gospel; he had to make sure that he and his congregation were putting it into practice.

18. *Philemon.* Although the letter to Philemon was supposed to be a personal communication on behalf of an escaped slave Onesimus, Paul's counsel on Christian fellowship makes it useful for all Christian readers.

19. *Hebrews.* This letter displays Jesus as God, human, high-priestly mediator, and the fulfillment of Jewish hopes.

20. *James.* James carries no central theme, but gives a series of practical, hard-hitting thrusts about living the Christian life.

21. *First Peter.* The letter contains miscellaneous exhortations and instructions to encourage new Christians to persevere in the faith in difficult times. Also, it shows how to apply the doctrines of Christianity in the duties of daily life.

22. *Second Peter.* This letter speaks out against false teachers and reminds believers that God had chosen them so they need to press forward.

23. *First John.* The writer dwells on the nature of Jesus Christ, his mission, and the principal doctrines of the Christian life. In several different ways, John made it clear that the real proof that we love God shows in the way we treat other people.

24. *Second John.* In this brief letter, John warns against the heresy of denying the incarnation and reminds his Christian friends to obey God's commandment of love.

25. *Third John.* John writes this letter to someone named Gaius, offering personal praise and advice.

26. *Jude.* Using pointed language and vivid images, this one-chapter book urges Christian friends to avoid false teachings. The writer appeals to the faithful to remember the teachings of the apostles.

27. *Revelation.* We cannot be certain precisely what all the mysterious pictures in this book mean. With his symbols, images, and numbers, John encourages believers of his own day, writes about the end of this age, and tells of the coming of the new Jerusalem. The book's powerful prophecy of the final happiness of the good and misery of the wicked makes it an unfailing source of warning and encouragement to Christians.

CHAPTER 32

Where Did the Bible Come From?

———— ∞ ————

Question: Where are the original manuscripts?

Answer: We don't know.

We can say this only about the *original manuscripts* because we don't have them. (The technical term for the original manuscripts is "autographs.")

If we don't have the originals, how can we be sure that the copies we have are still the Word of God? When the Old Testament writers finished their scrolls, there were no printing presses to duplicate their writing. They depended on scribes—men who copied the Scriptures patiently by hand when extra copies were needed or when the original scrolls became too worn to use. The first scribes attempted to make exact copies of the originals, and the scribes who followed them attempted to make exact copies of the copies. Even so, they didn't always avoid mechanical slips.

By the time Jesus was born, some Old Testament books had been copied and recopied over a span of nearly four hundred years. The books of the law, however, had been copied this way for more than twelve hundred years.

During that time, however, the scribes guarded the Old Testament text very well. It has been computed that, on the average, they mistakenly copied one word out of every 1,580. Even those mistakes were usually corrected when they made new copies.

Writers of the New Testament completed their manuscripts somewhere around A.D. 100. Being written in an age when literature flourished, and being copied constantly from the first days, the New Testament text has survived the centuries well. We have approximately fifteen thousand complete manuscripts and quotations of the New Testament today. All of them come from ancient sources, but none are original manuscripts.

The Inspired Book

First, let's do a historical overview of biblical texts. We have many fragments of the New Testament text that were written in the second century A.D. Some are on ostraka (scraps of pottery that early writers used as a cheap form of stationery) and talismans (pendants, bracelets, and other objects that early Christians wore to ward off evil spirits). Those objects contain only short quotations from the New Testament, so they give us little information about the original text.

More important are the papyrus manuscripts of the New Testament. Written on an early form of paper made from papyrus reeds, most of the manuscripts date from the third and fourth centuries A.D.

The earliest known fragment of a New Testament papyrus manuscript dates from about A.D. 125–140. This is commonly called the Rylands Fragment because it is housed in the John Rylands Library of Manchester, England. The fragment is only 2 1/2 x 3 1/4 inches, and it contains parts of John 18:32–33, 37–38. In spite of its early date, the fragment is too small to provide much information about the text of the Gospel of John in the second century.

Yet even without the original documents, Christians believe we have an extremely accurate text of the Bible. Through fragments and manuscripts that have been passed on, scholars have reconstructed a text that leaves little reason for doubt.

Most of the Old Testament was written in Hebrew and Aramaic (a form of Hebrew), and the New Testament was probably written entirely in Greek. (Some scholars think some of the writings were translated from the common language of the Jews—Aramaic—and then put into Greek.)

This brings us to ask: How can we trust the Bible today as being accurate?

That question still gets discussed. By comparing the most ancient manuscripts, there is a remarkable accuracy. Even the Dead Sea Scrolls support the accuracy of the Old Testament manuscripts.

We rely on the reality that the Bible has stood the test of time. For example, scoffers once laughed and said there were no Hittites in the ancient world. Then later archeological findings made it clear that they did exist and were quite prominent in history.

Those of the early church considered the inspiration of the Old Testament basic to its teaching about God. The New Testament books were still being written during the first century, so when New Testament writers referred to Scripture, they meant the books that we now know as the Old Testament. However, Paul specifically referred to the books of Moses as the old covenant in 2 Corinthians 3:13–15.

Paul wrote to Timothy, "All Scripture is God-breathed and is useful for teaching, rebuking, correcting and training in righteousness" (2 Tim. 3:16). Other verses, such as Hebrews 3:7 and 9:8, describe the Holy Spirit as speaking through the words of Scripture.

The Different Styles

"Wait a minute! If God inspired all this, then why does Paul sound different from Luke or Peter?"

Good question. I asked that myself when I was a new convert trying to understand inspiration.

Answer: God used individuals to write the Bible, and God also spoke to the world through their unique personalities. Many passages contain portions that reveal the author's previous training or temperamental experiences. For example, even if we didn't know that Luke was a medical man, we'd figure it out from his writing style. Quite naturally, he used medical terms—the vocabulary he normally used—and this also makes his writing quite difficult.

The story of Jesus' birth in Luke and the last two chapters of Acts are extremely difficult for most Greek readers. By contrast, John's writings, especially Revelation, are actually the simplest, easiest-to-read portions of the New Testament. (Yes, difficult to interpret, but even beginning Greek students can do quick reads of John's writings.)

This says an educated man wrote in much more complex ways than a lesser-educated person.

From the earliest days, the church has taught that God inspired every word in the Bible. A lot of people have argued over the idea of inspiration; a more modern idea says such things as, "God gave them their ideas, but they put them in their own words." Anyone holding that belief would have been kicked out of the church in the past.

Members of the early church firmly held that the Holy Spirit gave every single word in the original text to the writers. (We sometimes call this belief "verbal inspiration.") Yet the writing was never mechanical—that is, the writers didn't write as the Holy Spirit dictated each word. The human writers' thought processes weren't bypassed. Sometimes they didn't understand the things they wrote about—especially when it came to future events. Part of our spiritual legacy says that God so controlled (or inspired) the human authors that they couldn't introduce any defects into the writing, such as false history, inaccurate description, or misguided doctrine.

The position of the faithful church has always been that the present Bible of sixty-six books—aside from minor copyists' errors and mistranslations—is the very book that the Spirit of God designed for us.

From the most primitive days, the church has then gone on to say that the best way to understand the Bible is to read the Bible itself. That is, by comparing verses.

Also, along with this, Christians believe that the Bible contains everything necessary for salvation. This means that no denomination can impose or insist on any requirement for salvation that isn't found in the Bible.

For example, some groups have insisted that believers didn't belong to God until after they had been baptized. The Bible doesn't say that. Denominations like to speak of baptism as an act of obedience in following God. That's different from making baptism a requirement.

The Old Testament writers often insisted they were communicating God's Word. The prophets regularly introduced their statements with "Thus saith the Lord," "The word of the Lord that came unto me," or something similar. One scholar said that he found nearly four thousand such declarations in the Old Testament.

Christians are able to say, "We believe the Bible is the inspired, infallible Word of God." Once we make that statement, we are saying that not only do we trust the words of the Book, but we also trust the God who inspired the Book.

CHAPTER 33

Theology and Other Special Words

Can you imagine what it would have been like if a believer had come up to a follower of Roman gods and said, "If you want peace now and life everlasting after death, you need to believe in Jesus Christ"?

"Who is Jesus Christ? Why do I need to believe in him?" you might hear. "I worship the gods my parents taught me about. Why is your god better than mine?"

Such discussions pushed Christians to define their views and to clarify their understandings. We call such questions theology—a word that comes from the Greek (*Theos* = God, and *logos* = word). It means "the study of God and religious doctrines." Without a study of theology, we couldn't express much about what we believe.

"Who is Jesus Christ? Wasn't he just a man like everybody else?" These were some of the most significant questions to pour out of the pagan world. "How could he be God in a human form?" "What does it mean to be a Christian?" "What does it mean to believe?"

For centuries the sharpest minds in the church have discussed and argued among themselves as well as with those outside the faith. Slowly Christians accepted certain views as orthodox (Greek *orthos* = straight, and *doxa* = opinion or understanding) and the term came to mean "correct thinking."

In arriving at orthodox views, scholars had to find the words to explain what they meant. Sometimes theologians invented words such as Trinity or took already-known words such as *agape* (love) and reframed them with new meanings.

Since the beginning of the church, theologians have continued to seek better ways to communicate the faith of believers. In each generation different concerns emerge, and the church again attempts to communicate the faith more clearly.

The following words are theological terms that Christians use to express their faith. Many of these words aren't found in the Bible, and yet they are a vital part of Christian thinking. Most of us would have difficulty articulating what we believe without using them.

Age. This refers to an era or specific period of time during which certain related events come to pass. As used in the New Testament, the word generally refers to the present as opposed to the future. Paul calls Satan "the god of this age" (2 Cor. 4:4) and means that the age to come will belong to Jesus Christ.

Anoint or anointing. This was the practice of applying oil (olive, myrrh, balsam) or perfumed oil upon persons or things. It set apart a person for a special reason—for work, service, or healing. Terms such as "the LORD's anointed" are used of King Saul as a person set apart to serve God. David referred to him as the Lord's anointed and wouldn't harm him even when he had the opportunity.

The references most common in the Old Testament refer to the anointing of kings, prophets, and priests. In the New Testament, we find several references to anointing for healing, such as James 5:14.

Antichrist, the. This is the final opposition to Christ. The word appears only in the letters of John. As used there, the term referred to God's enemies in every age (see 1 John 2:18–29). Most Christians believe the Antichrist will be a person who will be the ultimate evil leader of the forces of evil against God.

Ark of the covenant. This was a sacred, portable chest in the Jewish tabernacle. It was the most important sacred object during the wilderness wanderings. For Jews, the ark was a symbol for the presence of God in their midst, like a portable throne for God.

Ascension, the. Fifty days after his resurrection, Jesus departed into heaven in the presence of his disciples. This event is described only in Acts 1:2–11. When he left, angels promised he would return.

Assurance. Assurance is an attitude of faith. It refers to the conviction, certainty, and unshakable confidence of believers that they are loved by God and that Jesus Christ has taken away their sins.

Baptism (Greek, *baptisma*). The word originally meant to wash, dip, or plunge something into water. Since the earliest days of the church, this rite has been used as the first outward, formal step of admission into God's church. Almost all Christians have practiced it since Jesus commanded his disciples to baptize. However, there are differences in the meaning and form of water baptism.

Three major positions on baptism exist among Christian groups.

1. *Sacramental view.* Baptism is a means by which God conveys grace. By undergoing this rite, those baptized receive remission of their sins, are regenerated (receive a new nature), and are given a new or strengthened faith. Roman Catholics and Lutherans hold this position.

2. *Covenant view.* Baptism is a sign and seal of the covenant—God's pledge to save the fallen race. The benefits of the covenant are for all adults who receive baptism, and are also for infants when parents make vows to teach them the faith. This brings children into the covenant, but they must themselves one day believe and make their own profession of faith. This is the view of Presbyterians and those of the Reformed faith.

3. *Symbolic view.* This position emphasizes the symbolic nature by emphasizing that baptism doesn't cause an inward change or change an individual's relationship to God. Baptism is a token—an outward indication—of inner changes that have already occurred in believers. This form of baptism is meant only for those who believe. It serves as a public identification of union with Jesus Christ and of the changes that have taken place. This makes baptism an act of obedience, commitment, and proclamation. Baptists, Charismatics, and Pentecostals hold this view.

The *form* of baptism has divided Christians into two major groups—those who insist upon the exclusive use of immersion and those who permit it but use other forms such as sprinkling or pouring.

Beatitudes. These are the declarations of blessedness made by Jesus at the beginning of the Sermon on the Mount in Matthew 5:3–12. Each begins with "Blessed are . . ." The Greek word translated as "blessed" means spiritual well-being.

Benediction. A prayer for God's blessings on the hearers. In Old Testament times, it was a regular part of the temple service. The most famous Old Testament benediction, called the Aaronic or the great high priestly blessing, occurs in Numbers 6:24–26: "The LORD bless you and keep you; the LORD make his face shine upon you and be gracious to you; the LORD turn his face toward you and give you peace."

Often called the apostolic benediction and used at the conclusion of many Christian worship services are the words from 2 Corinthians 13:14: "May the grace of the Lord Jesus Christ, and the love of God, and the fellowship of the Holy Spirit be with you all."

Blasphemy. A term that means to injure the reputation of another through cursing, slandering, and reviling. In the Bible, it means showing contempt or lack of reverence for God. It is also used of a person who claims divine attributes by word or deed (see Mark 14:64; John 16:33).

In the Old Testament, to blaspheme God was punishable by death, because it violated the third commandment by dishonoring the name of God.

Bless, blessing. The act of declaring, wishing, or praying for God's favor on others. In ancient days, people believed that the pronounced blessings had the power to bring them to pass.

Calvary. This word comes from the Latin and means "the skull." The NIV translates it as "the place called the Skull." It was the place where Jesus was crucified outside the city of Jerusalem. The word *Calvary* is often used to express the crucifixion.

Church. The Greek word *ekklesia* means "assembly" or "gathering." In the New Testament it always refers to a group such as all the Christians in a city (Acts 14:23) or those gathered for worship in a particular house (Rom. 16:5) or all Christians everywhere—the whole church (Matt. 16:18; Eph. 1:22). In the Bible, the word never identifies a building. Theologically, the word *church* refers to a local assembly of believers and includes the redeemed of all ages who follow Jesus Christ as Savior and Lord.

Coming. The Messiah or God's Anointed One coming to Israel for the final day of reckoning was a constant expectation of Old Testament prophets. Associated with the day of the LORD—the day when God would make all things right—was a messianic figure, a Davidic-type of king, or a suffering servant.

Some Jews found the statements about Messiah so baffling that they finally delineated two separate messiahs, one a king and the other a priest. Looking back, Christians grasp that God sent only one Messiah but in two comings. Jesus has come as a priest, a servant, a suffering Savior. He will return as a Davidic warrior and triumphant king.

The second coming of Jesus is the hope of believers through all the ages. Like those of old, we cannot see the end clearly from what God has revealed in the Bible. We cannot know for certain how and when the details will be filled in, but we know this much:

The appearing will be sudden and unexpected, like a thief who comes in the night (1 Thess. 5:1–3).

This momentous event will usher in the final judgment.

The resurrection of the dead will take place—everyone will be instantly changed, both the living and those who have already died (1 Cor. 15:51–54).

For Christians, this means being forever with Christ (1 Thess. 4:17).

Death. This is the end of either physical or spiritual life. Paul called death "the last enemy" (1 Cor. 15:26). He also taught that death entered the world as the result of sin, and that if there had been no sin, there would have been no death (see Rom. 5:17).

Death is more than a natural phenomenon: "The soul who sins is the one who will die" (Ezek. 18:4). When Paul described death as receiving the "wages of sin" (Rom. 6:23), he meant much more than its inevitable consequence. Death is God's verdict on human sinfulness.

Jesus Christ conquered death when he overcame sin by his crucifixion and resurrection. The Bible teaches that believers have already passed from death to life. Believers still face the weakness and pain that accompany physical dying, but they need not be afraid of death itself.

Dreams. In the Bible, dreams and visions were widely accepted as a means by which God speaks to individuals (for example, Jacob's dream in Gen. 28:12; Joseph's dreams in Gen. 37). Sometimes such dreams or visions were prophetic in nature.

Epiphany. This observance, of Eastern Orthodox origin, takes place on January 6. It occurs mostly in liturgical denominations, and it has a threefold reference: (1) the manifestation of Jesus to the world at his baptism (Mark 1:9); (2) Jesus changing water into wine at Cana (John 2:1–11); and (3) the visit of the Magi—which was added much later.

Eternal life. The term refers to the quality of new existence in Christ, as well as its unending character that begins in this life. It is surprising for many people to learn that in ancient Israel there was no serious evidence of belief in life after death until after the return from exile in Babylon (see Dan. 12:1–2). By New Testament times, eternal life had become an accepted understanding, especially among Christians after the resurrection of Jesus.

Most New Testament references to eternal life are oriented to the future and emphasize the quality of the life that will be enjoyed endlessly. Eternal life is a gift of God to all who believe in Jesus Christ.

Eternal punishment. An essential teaching of the New Testament is that God punishes sinners who don't repent. This punishment is an everlasting punishment (see John 5:28–29; Rom. 5:12–21).

Evangelical. Originally this was a technical term that came into use during the Protestant Reformation as a means of self-identification. It signified belief in two important doctrines: (1) justification by faith and (2) the ultimate authority of the Bible.

Eventually the term *evangelical* narrowed and now refers to those who hold to fundamental doctrines and emphasize personal conversion, a moral life, and a zeal for spreading the Christian faith.

Faith. In the Bible, the word *faith* (or trust or belief) means to put trust in or reliance on the one who alone is trustworthy. It occurs frequently in the Bible, expressing the acceptable attitude of God's people toward their loving Creator. In the New Testament, faith is not merely to accept or agree; it implies active obedience (see Rom. 10:16).

Fall. The Fall refers to the disobedience and sin of Adam and Eve, as well as the results of disobedience that caused them to lose the state of innocence in which they had been created. That event plunged them and all of humanity into a state of sin and corruption. The account of the Fall appears in Genesis 3.

Fellowship. The word refers to a communal association for mutual benefit. Essentially a New Testament emphasis, it is the bond among Christians created by their common confession that Jesus Christ is Lord. Fellowship binds together, and its primary emphasis is on encouraging and sharing with others.

Forgiveness. In the Old Testament, the word meant "to cover, remove, or wipe away." The Bible vividly records human sinfulness, God's eagerness to forgive, and frequent calls by the prophets and leaders, and later by Jesus and his followers, to repent from and accept God's forgiveness.

In the New Testament, God forgives sins through the death of Jesus Christ. This forgiveness is described in several ways, especially as justification, salvation, and reconciliation. Forgiveness lies at the heart of Christianity. A right relationship with God is the basic human need. Because sin is primarily an offense against God, it is God who forgives.

Gospel. The gospel is the good news—the literal meaning of the Greek word—and refers specifically to the Good

News of the death, burial, and resurrection of Jesus Christ as preached by the disciples (see 1 Cor. 15:1–4). The offer of the gospel is forgiveness and freedom from sin on the basis of faith in Jesus Christ (see Eph. 2:8–9).

Grace. This is God's kindness toward humanity, shown without regard to the worth or merit of those who receive it and in spite of what they deserve. Through this grace, we become members of Christ's body (1 Cor. 12:27) and partakers of the divine nature (2 Pet. 1:4).

Guilt. This word and other forms of it (guilty, guiltiness) occur about thirty times in the Bible. For biblical writers, it's not primarily an inward feeling, remorse, or a bad conscience, but guilt involves the result of sin committed against God or others.

Guilt is based on two understandings. First, human beings are responsible and accountable for their actions, thoughts, and attitudes. Second, these actions, thoughts, and attitudes constitute a state of guilt when the relationship between human beings and God or other people have been broken because of sin.

Heaven. The word has three uses in the Bible:

- In a physical sense, heaven is the expanse over the earth (Gen. 1:8).
- Heaven, as the top layer of a three-story universe, refers to the dwelling place of God (Gen. 28:17).
- Heaven as a substitute for the name of God (see Luke 15:8–21; John 3:27). The kingdom of God and the kingdom of heaven are often spoken of interchangeably (Matt. 4:17).

For many people, heaven is a general term that refers to the final place for all Christians. A better term for this is the new heavens and the new earth mentioned in Revelation 21:1.

Hell. This is the dreaded place of eternal punishment for the unrighteous. Some versions use this word to translate *sheol* (Hebrew) and *hades* (Greek), both of which refer to the place or abode of the dead.

Hell as a place of punishment translates *gehenna,* the Greek form of the Hebrew word that means the "vale of Hinnom"—a valley south of Jerusalem. In that valley the Canaanites worshiped Baal and the fire god Molech by sacrificing their children in fire that burned continuously. Jesus spoke of hell *(gehenna)* as a place of outer darkness and a furnace of fire, where there will be wailing, weeping, and gnashing of teeth (see Matt. 8:12; 13:42, 50; 25:30; Luke 13:28).

Holy, holiness. In the Old Testament, *holiness* means to separate from the ordinary and implies a connection with God. Thus, God is holy. People, things, and actions may be made or declared holy because of their association with God. Holiness also includes the idea of consecration to God and purification from what is evil or improper.

Like Israel in the Old Testament, the church is holy (even though imperfect). Paul refers to believers as "saints" (that is, the holy ones; Rom. 1:7; 1 Cor. 1:2).

Hope. This is not merely wishing, but the sense of confident expectation of good from God. It also refers to the second coming of Jesus Christ.

Idolatry. The worship of something created as opposed to worshiping the Creator. Idolatry was probably the greatest temptation the Israelites faced in the wilderness. So serious was the sin that making or worshiping any image was prohibited as the second of the Ten Commandments. Only after the Jews returned from Babylon does there appear to be no serious temptation to worship idols.

Incarnation. This is the Christian doctrine that the pre-existent Son of God became human in Jesus. The word doesn't appear in the Bible, but it's part of the foundation of belief in the virgin birth and the resurrection of Jesus.

Lots, casting of. This was a way of making decisions in Bible times, similar to drawing straws to determine the course of action to be taken. Faith in God working through this method meant the people didn't question its use. They usually asked a yes/no question. There are seventy references to this practice in the Old Testament and seven in the New Testament.

Love. Two different Greek words for *love* appear in the New Testament. (1) *Phileo,* often used for "friendship," means "to be fond of," "to have affection for." This is a word of emotion or feelings. (2) *Agape* means to esteem or have high regard for, but it's an attitude or a commitment, not an emotion. This is the characteristic word used by Christians.

Miracles. This refers to any special interventions by God. Often they are historic events or natural phenomena that appear to violate natural laws. The Bible commonly uses *sign* to denote miracles that point to deeper meanings behind the acts themselves. Another word, *wonder,* emphasizes the effect of the miracle that brings awe or even terror to the beholder.

Mystery. The New Testament use of *mystery* refers to God's plan that has previously not been revealed. Paul uses the word several times and means not only a previously hidden truth that is presently divulged but one that contains a supernatural element that remains in the spirit of the revelation.

Obey or Obedience. This word ties together hearing *and* obeying. Obedience signifies an active response to something heard rather than passive listening.

Parable. Parables are short, simple stories with a double meaning. Today we would label them as metaphors. These are truths illustrated by a comparison or example drawn from everyday experience. Jesus often taught through parables. The two most famous parables are the lost (or prodigal) son in Luke 15:11–32 and the good Samaritan in Luke 10:25–37. Both parables condemn the self-righteous and illustrate God's love and compassion.

Proverb. A short, popular saying that communicates a familiar truth or observation in an expressive or easily remembered form.

Redemption. Deliverance by payment of a price. In the New Testament, this term refers to salvation through the death of Jesus Christ.

Repentance. The word has several meanings in the Old Testament, from regret to changing the mind. In the New Testament, however, it refers to a turning from sin and toward God. Several times people are called to repentance, such as during the preaching of John the Baptist or Peter on the day of Pentecost.

Repentance is bound up with faith and is inseparable from it. Without some measure of faith, no one truly repents.

Resurrection. Being raised from the dead. Resurrection has three primary meanings in the Bible:

1. *Miraculous healings.* These were individuals who were brought back to life in this present world, such as the widow's son by Elijah (1 Kings 17:20–24). They eventually died again.

2. *Jesus' resurrection.* This resurrection is linked with the overcoming of the powers of evil and death. Jesus' resurrection is the basis for the doctrine of general resurrection (1 Cor. 15:12–19).

3. *General resurrection.* The New Testament teaches the resurrection of all believers based on Jesus being the first one risen from the dead (1 Cor. 15:12–58). Believers are resurrected to life and unbelievers to eternal punishment.

Resurrection is physical. It's more than resuscitation of the physical body; it's a complete transformation. We don't know exactly what those resurrected bodies will be like, but we do know our bodies will be:

• recognizable,
• those in which the spirit dominates,
• unlimited by physical boundaries,
• eternal bodies, and
• "glorious" bodies (see Rom. 8:18; 1 Cor. 15:43).

Righteousness. Purity of heart—being and doing right. Righteousness comes as a gift by faith in Jesus Christ (2 Cor. 5:21) and not from obeying the Law of Moses.

Sacraments. A formal religious act in which the actions and materials used are the channels or means by which God communicates grace—actually or symbolically. The word never appears in the Bible. Roman Catholics and the Orthodox have seven sacraments (Lord's Supper or

Eucharist, baptism, confirmation, repentance or forgiveness of sins, matrimony, holy orders, and extreme unction or anointing of those in danger of death). Protestant Christians sometimes prefer to call them ordinances, and they recognize only baptism and the Lord's Supper as sacraments. Their reasoning is that only these two rites were instituted and commanded by Jesus.

Salvation. The English word stands for several Hebrew and Greek words, the general idea being safety, deliverance, ease, and soundness. In the Old Testament, the word *salvation* had many uses, such as deliverance from danger, healing from sickness, or national deliverance from military threat.

In the New Testament, salvation finds its deepest meaning in the substitutionary death and resurrection of Jesus Christ. Human need for salvation is one of the clearest teachings of the Bible.

Scapegoat. On the Day of Atonement, the high priest brought out a live goat over whose head he confessed all the sins of the Israelites. The goat was then sent into the wilderness, symbolically taking away their sins. This process represented the transfer of guilt from the people to the animal. The scapegoat is a *type* of Christ.

Sermon on the Mount. This is the title given to Jesus' moral and ethical teachings as recorded only in Matthew 5 through 7. The Beatitudes are the best-known section. It also contains the Golden Rule: "In everything, do to others what you would have them do to you" (Matt. 7:12).

Speaking in tongues. The act of speaking in a language either unknown or incomprehensible to the speaker. This phenomenon played a prominent role in the life of early

Christianity and is described in Acts 2 (see also Acts 19:1–6).

Tabernacle. A specially designed tent that served as a place of worship for the nation of Israel during their early history. King Solomon built the temple as a permanent place of worship.

Temple. When the Bible speaks of the temple, it refers to Solomon's temple—the first permanent place of worship for Israel. The Babylonians destroyed the temple (about 586/7 B.C), and it was rebuilt after the Jews returned from Babylon. The second temple was destroyed about 167 B.C by the Syrians and rebuilt by Herod the Great. After the Romans destroyed the temple in A.D. 70, it was never rebuilt.

Temptation. An enticement to do evil, although the Bible uses the word in two different senses. The first use is testing or proving by a test to determine the depth and integrity of commitment to God. Abraham was tested by God to sacrifice his son. In the New Testament, persecution is called a testing (as in 1 Pet. 1:3–9). The intent of such testing is ultimately to strengthen faith and devotion to God.

The second, more common meaning, is to entice to sin with the implied promise of greater good to be derived from following the way of disobedience. The Bible makes it clear, as in James 1:12–15, that God doesn't tempt humans to do evil.

Type. This nonbiblical word refers to a figure, representation, or symbol of something to come. Usually, it's an Old Testament event that foreshadows something of a deeper meaning in the New Testament. Most types find their fulfillment in the person and ministry of Jesus Christ.

Examples of typology are the work and actions of Melchizedek, the king-priest of Salem (Gen. 14:18–20), who is said to foreshadow Christ (Heb. 6:20). Jesus said in John 3:14–15 that the brazen serpent in the wilderness (Num. 21:4–9) was a type of his own crucifixion. The innocent scapegoat symbolically took upon itself the sins of the people of Israel, and is a type of Christ.

Visions. These were experiences, similar to dreams, and brought about spiritual insight or awareness, given by divine revelation. Dreams occur while asleep and visions while awake. People who had visions were filled with a special consciousness of God. The most notable in the Old Testament were Ezekiel and Daniel. In the New Testament, visions are prominent in Luke, Acts, and Revelation.

CHAPTER 34

Where It All Ends

When and how is all of history going to end? Today, many people seek answers to the events of the end time. Perhaps this may be the natural result of grappling with issues such as space exploration, genetic engineering, and the expanding number of nations around the globe that now manufacture their own nuclear weapons.

And yet our age isn't all that different from others. Ever since Jesus Christ ascended into heaven, Christians have awaited his return. And as they have waited they have raised questions about eschatology—the study of last things.

Among Christians, certain events are universally accepted:

- the visible and bodily return of Jesus Christ (called rapture by some),
- the judgment of all people, and
- the creation of the new heavens and the new earth where all the righteous will remain forever.

The biggest disagreement has to do with the timing and the details of those three events. Prior to the mid-nineteenth century, the church as a whole saw the end of time in the following sequence:

1. Jesus Christ would return to the earth.

2. This return would usher in the destruction of the present world.

3. All nations and individuals would stand in judgment before God.

4. All people would be sent to eternal bliss or damnation, depending on their behavior and faith in Jesus Christ.

With the rise of dispensationalism, around 1850, which was popularized by the Scofield Reference Bible in the early years of the twentieth century, a different theological position emerged. While others take many of the terms symbolically, such as the great tribulation, dispensationalists consider this a literal period of seven years.

Generally speaking, dispensationalists see the end of the world in the following sequence:

- The return of Jesus Christ—the rapture—when God's people will be snatched or seized from the earth.

- The great tribulation of seven years' duration will take place on the earth while the church is gone.

- Jesus and believers will return at the end of the seven years and set up a rule on earth that will last one thousand years—the millennium.

- At the end of that period, Satan and his army will rise up in a final-but-futile war—the battle of Armageddon.

- Jesus Christ and the angels of heaven will cast Satan into the lake of fire.

- Then follow the judgments—first, that of separating
  the righteous and the unrighteous (Matt. 24:31–39),
  and second, the judgment of the great white throne
  (2 Cor. 5:10) where believers receive their rewards.

Note: The second judgment of the great white throne is
only for Christians.

∞

Because of the differing viewpoints on three items above
(the rapture, the great tribulation, and the millennium),
more detailed explanations follow.

The Rapture

Derived from the Latin *apio,* the term *rapture* has two
basic meanings. First, it means "to seize," such as the
ecstasy of spirit mystics sometimes enjoy. The second
meaning is "to snatch" or "a removal from one place to
another by forcible means."

In eschatology, the word is used only in this second
sense, as a phase of the prophetic revelation dealing with
the future coming of the Lord for the church.

Paul sought to comfort believers at Thessalonica whose
loved ones had recently died with the assurance that at the
return of Jesus Christ these would be given first consideration. When they were raised, the living saints would be
caught up together with them in the clouds to meet the
Lord in the air, never to be separated from him or from
one another (see 1 Thess. 4:17).

The Great Tribulation

As stated above, dispensationalists believe in a literal
and intense period of distress and suffering at the end of

time. The exact phrase, the "great tribulation," is found only once in the Bible (Rev. 7:14). They distinguish the great tribulation from general tribulations and trials that confront believers in the world through all periods of human history.

There are three different views among dispensationalists concerning the relation of the second coming of Christ to the tribulation period.

Pretribulationists, the most generally held view, puts the rapture before the tribulation. They believe that the pouring out of the divine wrath upon a Christ-rejecting society marks this seven-year period. Advocates of this view believe that God has promised to exempt the church from this horrific trouble and judgment that is coming upon the entire world. The rapture is God's way of fulfilling that purpose.

Midtribulationists hold that the church will be on earth during the first half of the seven years. Only the latter half will be marked by tribulation, preceded by a period of peace and safety. The saints will be spared the ordeal of tribulation, and the rapture will occur at this midway point. In substance, this view doesn't differ much from the preceding, because both maintain the exemption of the church from the tribulation era.

Posttribulationists believe that the church will remain on the earth during the predicted time of trouble and wrath. Although few hold to this belief, most of them believe God's people will receive a mark to protect them—again, this is similar in that the church is spared.

For posttribulationists, no interval will occur between the rapture and the coming of the Lord with the resurrected saints to judge the world and set up the thousand-year kingdom.

The Millennium

Dispensationalists also take this literally as the thousand-year period mentioned in connection with the description of Christ's coming to reign with believers over the earth (see Rev. 20).

They teach that during this thousand-year period, the faithful who have died for Christ will be resurrected before the millennium and all believers will rule with Christ on earth. Satan will be bound in a bottomless pit so he can't deceive the nations again until after the thousand years. He will then be released to resume his work of deceit before being overpowered by Jesus.

The most important aspect of the millennium is the reign of Christ. Then all of God's enemies will be wiped out.

There are three viewpoints on the thousand-year reign of Christ.

Premillennialism, the view held by dispensationalists, as discussed above, teaches that this age will end in judgment at the return of Jesus Christ, who will restore the kingdom of Israel and reign for one thousand years. The millennium will be the last of the ordered ages of time, followed by Satan's short-lived revolt, and then will come the dawning of eternity.

Amillennialism or *nonmillennialism* holds that the millennium refers to Christ's *spiritual* rule today from heaven. They point out that if we take the six references to the word *millennium* in Revelation 20 literally (see vv. 2–7), no other portion of the New Testament speaks about a literal reign upon earth of one thousand years. The rest of Revelation 20 is filled with symbols that cannot be taken literally (e.g., the bottomless pit and the great chain, v. 1). Further, a literal interpretation would be contrary to the usual use of the word *thousand,* as in 2 Peter 3:8.

The reign of Christ on earth, amillennialists say, is taking place now. Spiritually Christ has defeated Satan and holds ultimate power. The millennial reign ends when Jesus Christ returns for all believers, and this ushers in the events of eternity.

Another similar group views everything in Revelation 1–20 as historical and symbolic. That is, they teach that most of the Book of Revelation was happening primarily during the period of Roman rule. John wrote in his unusual style so that the enemies of the church wouldn't understand. For them, only the last two chapters are futuristic.

Postmillennialism, held by relatively few, was a popular position before World War I and World War II. It views Christ's spiritual rule as working through preaching and teaching to bring a gradual world improvement that leads up to Christ's return. This position has been largely abandoned.

∞

So where does it all end? No one really knows. We have hints and pictures, but we don't know the ultimate reality. For example, John wrote, "There will be no more night. They will not need the light of a lamp or the light of the sun, for the Lord God will give them light" (Rev. 22:5). Few serious biblical students take these pictures literally.

They are written symbolically because they defy explanation. John had moments of insight that defied putting into words. He wrote his books in the only way humanity could grasp—the use of symbols that readers would understand.

Where does it all end? No matter which eschatological position any of us holds to, God's ultimate reality is going to surpass it anyway.

The Bible assures us that all believers will be with Jesus Christ and that this experience will be far greater than anything human minds could have contemplated.

In the meantime, here are John's last words, and the very last words of the Bible, which are given as a benediction:

"The grace of the Lord Jesus be with God's people. Amen" (Rev. 22:21).

Amen.